500 CHILDREN'S SERMON OUTLINES

JOHN RITCHIE

KREGEL PUBLICATIONS
Grand Rapids, Michigan 49501

500 Children's Sermon Outlines by John Ritchie.
Copyright © 1987 by Kregel Publications, a division of
Kregel, Inc. All rights reserved.

Library of Congress Cataloging-in-Publication Data

Ritchie, John, 1853-1930.
  500 Children's Sermon Outlines.

  Reprint. Originally published: Five Hundred Children's
Subjects, 2nd ed., rev. and enl. Kilmarnock, Scotland:
J. Ritchie, 1911.
  Includes index.
  1. Bible — Outlines, syllabi, etc. 2. Children's sermons.
I. Title. II. Title: Five hundred children's subjects.
BS591.R57   1987   251'.02   86-27396
ISBN 0-8254-3623-0

1 2 3 4 5 Printing/Year 91 90 89 88 87

Printed in the United States of America

CONTENTS

PUBLISHER'S PREFACE

"Preach the Word" was the admonition that Paul gave to the young preacher, Timothy (2 Tim. 4:2). What was so essential 2000 years ago is still necessary today. To "preach the Word" is to expound Scripture truths with clarity and conviction.

The *John Ritchie Sermon Outline* series has helped many to preach effectively since they were first published. Based on Scripture portions, these outlines bring out truths that change lives and minister to present needs. These aids are not intended to diminish a personal, prayerful study of the Bible. Rather, they will encourage it by giving insights to those who preach or teach God's truths.

These brief sermon outlines will enlighten, instruct and give direction to the believer as he walks the path marked out in the Word. They will also refresh and strengthen the inner man in his desire to better know God's word.

For the busy preacher or lay person who needs stimulating ideas for a dynamic preaching or teaching ministry, these sermon outlines will be most beneficial.

PREFACE

The five hundred children's outlines found in these pages, have been gathered from the Word of God and used in making known the glad tidings of God's redeeming love among young folks, during a period of forty years. They are now passed on for the aid of fellow-workers, who may need a helping hand to fill their seed baskets with "good seed" to sow new fields, their scrips with "smooth stones" to slay giants stalking through the land, and their quivers with "sharp arrows" to wing their way straight to the conscience and the heart. They are not intended to diminish, but rather to encourage prayerful scripture study and personal acquaintance with the Sacred Word.

The "subjects" are simple, the "outlines" natural, and the "notes" only suggestive, the preacher or the teacher being best able to fit in and fill up with that which will meet the need of those to whom he bears the message.

Hallowed memories of times of awakening, seasons of revival, days of ingathering, with first testimonies of newborn souls to God's saving grace, come to mind in connection with these subjects and their use in children's meetings and Sunday schools when the Gospel in its love and power was used by the Spirit to bring life to the dead, pardon to the guilty, and peace to the troubled.

SIMPLE GOSPEL TRUTHS

1   **The Gospel**

Its Message (1 Cor. 15:1)—Declared
Its Power (Rom. 1:16)—Manifested
Its Receivers (Acts 11:21)—Converted
Its Effects (Acts 8:8)—Enjoyed

2   **Two Welcomings**

"They welcomed Him" (Luke 8:40)
"He welcomed them" (Luke 9:11)

> So now some sinners receive Christ (John 1:12)
> And so now Christ receives sinners (Luke 15:2)

3   **Seeking**

A sinner seeking the Savior (Luke 19:2, 9)
The Savior seeking a sinner (John 4:1, 8)

> He seeks and saves (Luke 19:10)
> Sinners receive and rejoice (Luke 19:6)

4   **Three Stages**

"Without Christ"—By Nature (Eph. 2:12)
"In Christ"—By Grace (Eph 2:13)
"With Christ"—In Glory (Phil. 1:23)

> Out of self, into Christ, into Glory

5   Forgiveness of Sins
Promised (Acts 26:18)—In the Word
Proclaimed (Acts 13:38)—In the Gospel
Possessed (Eph. 1:7)—In the Soul

6   Three Confessions of Christ
"My Savior" (Luke 1:47)—By Mary
"My Lord" (Phil. 3:8)—By Paul
"My God" (John 20:28)—By Thomas

7   Christ's Invitations
"Come unto Me" (Matt. 11:28)—For Rest
"Abide in Me" (John 15:3)—For Fruitfulness
"Follow Me" (Matt. 9:19)—For Service

8   Whosoevers
The "Whosoever" of Salvation (John 3:16)
The "Whosoever" of Forgiveness (Acts 10:43)
The "Whosoever" of Regeneration (1 John 5:1)
The "Whosoever" of Condemnation (Rev. 20:15)

9   God's Salvation
His own arm brought it (Isa. 63:5)
His Gospel proclaims it (Eph. 1:13)
His Grace imparts it (Eph. 2:8)
His People possess it (Phil. 2:12)

10   The Gospel
Of Peace to the Troubled (Rom. 10:15)
Of Salvation to the Lost (Eph. 1:13)
Of Grace to the Guilty (Acts 20:24)

11 **Salvation for All**
God's Love is for "the World" (John 3:16)
Christ's Ransom is "for all" (1 Tim. 2:6)
The Gospel is to "every creature" (Mark 16:15)
The Invitation is to "Whosoever will" (Rev. 22:17)

12 **Christ for Me**
I Receive Him as Savior (John 1:12)
I Confess Him as Lord (Rom. 10:9)
I Follow Him as Shepherd (Ps. 23:1)
I Learn of Him as Teacher (Matt. 11:29)

13 **Behold**
Behold ye have sinned (Num. 32:23)—Condemnation
Behold the Lamb of God (John 1:29)—Substitution
Behold now is the day (2 Cor. 5:12)—Grace
Behold He cometh (Rev. 1:7)—Judgment

14 **Christ Is All**
Christ dying on the Cross—The Believer's Savior
   (1 Peter 2:24)
Christ living on the Throne—The Believer's Object
   (Heb. 12:2)
Christ coming to the Air—The Believer's Hope (Titus
   2:13)

15 **Some Scripture "I Wills"**
I will Arise (Luke 15:18)—Repentance
I will Trust (Isa. 12:2)—Faith
I will Take (Ps. 116:13)—Salvation
I will Sing (Ps. 52:9)—Praise

16   Spiritual Life

Life manifested in the Son (John 1:2)
Life imparted by the Father (1 John 5:11)
Life sustained by the Word (1 Peter 2:2)
Life strengthened by the Spirit (Rom. 8:2)

17   Lips

The Sinner's Lips—Unclean (Isa. 6:5)
The Believer's Lips—Purged (Isa. 6:6)
The Worshiper's Lips—Praising (Heb. 13:15)
The Witness' Lips—Testifying (Prov. 15:7)

18   Messages From Olivet

The Place of Christ's Loneliness (John 8:1)
  —Humiliation
The Place of Christ's Tears (Luke 19:41, 44)
  —Compassion
The Scene of Christ's Agony (Matt. 26:30)—Suffering
The Scene of Christ's Ascension (Acts 1:12)—Glory
The Place of Christ's Return (Zech. 14:4)—Reign

19   Prayer and Promise

	Prayer	Promise
Cleanse Me	(Ps. 51:2)	(John 15:3)
Keep Me	(Ps. 67:8)	(1 Sam. 2:9)
Guide Me	(Ps. 31:3)	(Ps. 32:8)
Receive Me	(Ps. 49:15)	(John 14:3)

20   Past, Present, Future

What I *was* (Rom. 5:10)—God's Enemy
What I *am* (1 John 3:1)—God's Child
What I *shall be* (Rom. 8:17)—God's Heir

21   Good News

A Call to the Thirsty (John 7:37)—Come and Drink

An Invitation to the Hungry (John 21:12)—Come and Dine

A Request to the Weary (Matt. 11:28)—Come and Rest

22   Feet

The Sinner's Feet (Prov. 1:16)—Run in Sin

The Savior's Feet (Ps. 22:16)—Pierced for Sin

The Saved One's Feet (Ps. 40:2)—Set on a Rock

The Servant's Feet (Isa. 52:7; Eph. 6:15)—Shod to Run

23   All the World

Love for all the World (John 3:16)

A Savior for all Men (1 Tim. 2:4, 6)

A Gospel to every Creature (Matt. 16:15)

24   For Whom Christ Gave Himself

For All (1 Tim. 2:6)—Universal

For the Church (Eph. 5:25)—Special

For Us (Eph. 5:2)—Individual

For Me (Gal. 2:20)—Personal

25   Steps in the Heavenly Life

Washed from Sin (Rev. 1:7)—In Christ's Blood

Walking in New Life (Rom. 6:4)—In Christ's Power

Working for Other's Good (Col. 3:13)—In Christ's Name

Waiting in Hope (1 Thess. 1:10)—For Christ's Coming

The order given is right—Salvation first, service next.

26 Divine Invitations

Come to the Waters (Isa. 55:1)—To the Thirsty
Come, let us Reason (Isa. 1:18)—To the Guilty
Come, and I will give Rest (Matt. 11:28)—To the Weary

27 Small Beginnings

A Small Seed (Mark 4:31)—Became a Great Tree
A Little Leaven (Matt. 13:33)—Permeated the Whole
A Few Loaves (Matt. 14:17)—Fed a Multitude

> So are the beginnings of sin, evil doctrine, wrong-doing,
> grace in the heart, new life at conversion, leading on to
> endless glory or woe.

28 A Threefold Cord

An Earnest Appeal—"Blot out mine iniquities"
(Ps. 51:9)
An Accomplished Work—"Laid on Him the iniquity of
us all" (Isa. 53:6)
A Glorious Result—"Whose iniquities are forgiven"
(Rom. 4:7)

29 Things Everlasting

Everlasting Life (Rom. 6:22)—To Enjoy
Everlasting Light (Isa. 41:7)—To Walk in
Everlasting Love (Jer. 31:3)—To Abide in

30 Certainties

True of all who now believe in Christ

Shall not come into Condemnation (John 5:24)
Shall never Perish (John 10:28)
Shall not see Death (John 8:51)

31   Certainties

Sure to all unbelievers and the ungodly

Shall not see Life (John 3:36)
Shall be Damned (Mark 16:16)
Shall go into Punishment (Mark 25:47)

32   From Rags to a Robe

Rags Unclean (Isa. 64:5)—Human Righteousness
Garments Patched (Mark 2:21)—Man's Reformation
The Best Robe (Luke 15:22)—God's Righteousness

    1. All that belongs to sinners by nature
    2. All that man can do by practice
    3. What God gives in grace

33   "The Whole World"

Lieth in Wickedness (1 John 5:19)—Degradation
Deceived by Satan (Rev. 20:3, 10)—Infatuation
Guilty before God (Rom. 3:19)—Condemnation
Christ's Death avails for (1 John 2:2)—Salvation

34   My Life Story

I was born at Ephesians 2:2
I lived in Titus 3:3
I heard of a wonderful gift in John 3:16
I saw a great sight in John 1:29
I received a great possession in 1 John 5:12
I am now in a good position in Romans 8:1
I expect soon to be leaving for 1 Thessalonians 4:17

35   Tenses of Life

I *was* "without Christ" (Eph. 2:12)
I *am* "in Christ" (Rom. 8:1)
I *shall be* "like Christ" (1 John 3:2)

36   The Christian Athlete

The Entrance (John 10:9)—Conversion
The Stripping (Heb. 12:1)—Separation
The Course (Phil. 3:14)—Progression
The Goal (2 Tim. 4:9)—Glorification

37   What Is Ready?

The Sinner is Ready to Perish (Isa. 27:13)
The Salvation of God is Ready (Luke 14:17)
The Evangelist is Ready to Preach (Rom. 1:15)
God is Ready to Pardon (Neh. 9:17)

38   Divine Forgiveness

As proclaimed to all in Acts 13:38

Its Ground—The Blood of Christ (Eph. 1:7)
Its Source—The Grace of God (Eph. 1:7)
Its Extent—All Trespasses (Col. 2:13)

39   "To the Uttermost"

Wrath on the Unbeliever (1 Thess. 2:17)
Salvation to the Believer (Heb. 7:25)
The Gospel to be Preached (Acts 1:8)
Retribution to the Ungodly (Matt. 5:26)

40   The Right Hand of God

Where Christ is at present

A Place of Rest—He "sat down" (Heb. 10:12)
A Place of Honor—"Exalted to be a Prince" (Acts 5:31)
A Place of Reward—"He Despised the Shame" (Heb. 12:2)
A Place of Service—"An High Priest" (Heb. 8:1)

41   Four Great Gospel Facts

Christ *died* for our sins (1 Cor. 15:3)
He was *raised* for our Justification (Rom. 4:25)
He ever *liveth* to make Intercession (Rom. 8:34)
He will *come* again to receive us (John 14:3)

42   Christ's Gifts to Us

He giveth His Life for the Sheep (John 10:15)
He gives His Peace to His People (John 14:27)
He gives His Word to His Disciples (John 17:14)
He gives strength to the Weak (2 Cor. 12:9)
He will give Glory to all His own (Ps. 84:11)

43   Two Decisions

"I will go" (Gen. 24:45)
"I will not go" (Num. 10:30)

> Rebekah's choice is like the soul accepting Christ
> Hobab's refusal is like the Christ rejecter

44   Opened

Ears to hear the Word (Isa. 1:4)
Scriptures to make it known (Luke 24:32)
Understanding to perceive it (Luke 24:45)
Heart to receive it (Acts 16:14)
Lips to confess it (Ps. 51:15)

45   The Sinner's Attitude Toward God

Ears stopped, not to hear the Word (Zech. 7:11)
Eyes closed, against the Light (Acts 28:27)
Back turned to God (Jer. 2:27)

46   Three Great "Beholds"

"Behold the Man" (John 19:5)—For Scorn
"Behold the Lamb" (John 1:29)—For Salvation
"Behold My Hands" (John 20:27)—For Peace

47   Five "Faithful Sayings"

Of the Sinner's Salvation (1 Tim. 1:15)
Of the Saint's Sanctification (1 Tim. 4:11)
Of the Worker's Service (1 Tim. 3:1)
Of the Believer's Standard (Titus 3:8)
Of the Christian's Suffering (2 Tim. 2:11)

48   Now

Now is the day of Salvation (2 Cor. 6:2)
Now the time of Justification (Rom. 5:9)
Now there is no Condemnation (Rom. 8:1)

49   How God Disposes of Sins

He laid them upon the Sin-bearer (Isa. 53:6)
He forgives them to the Believer (Eph. 1:7)
He blots them out of His sight (Isa. 44:22)
He removes them far away (Ps. 103:12)
He casts them behind His back (Micah 7:19)
He remembers them no more (Heb. 10:17)

50   Great Manifestations

Life was manifested in Christ's path (1 John 1:5)
Love was manifested in Christ's death (1 John 4:9)
Light was manifested in Christ's resurrection (2 Tim. 1:10)
Long-suffering is manifested in Christ's enthronement
   (2 Peter 3:9)

51   Full Redemption

"By Christ" at the Cross (1 Peter 1:19)
"In Christ" on the Throne (Rom. 3:24)
"With Christ" at His coming (Rom. 8:23)

52   The Man, Christ Jesus

The testimony of many witnesses

The Officers: "Never man spake like this Man" (John 7:46)
The Robber: "This Man hath done nothing amiss" (Luke 23:41)
The Scribes: "This Man receiveth sinners" (Luke 15:2)
The Centurion: "This was a righteous Man" (Luke 23:47)
The People: "We will not have this Man" (Luke 19:14)
The Doorkeeper: "Art thou one of this Man's disciples?" (John 18:17)

53   Looking Unto Jesus

As the Savior, lifted up (Isa. 45:22; John 3:14)
As the Forerunner, Glorified (Heb. 12:2)
As the Example, Walking (John 1:36)
As the Hope, Coming (Titus 2:13)

54   Three Striking Facts

"Without shedding of *blood*" there is no *coming* to God (Heb. 9:22)
"Without *faith*" there is no *pleasing* of God (Heb. 11:6)
"Without *holiness*" there is no *seeing* of God (Heb. 12:14)

55   Christ's Three Crowns

Of Thorns (John 19:2)—The Cross
Of Glory (Heb. 2:9)—The Throne
Of Kingly Power (Rev. 19:9)—The Kingdom

The first was a Crown of Mockery
The second is a Crown of Victory
The third is a Diadem of Power

56   A True Christian

Is made so by receiving and confessing Christ

By Persuasion, he is Converted (Acts 26:29)
By Calling, he is Named (Acts 11:26)
By Suffering, he is Proved (1 Peter 4:16)

These are the only passages in which the word appears.

57   Dead

Dead *in* Sin (Eph. 2:1)—The Sinner's State
Dead *for* Sin (1 Cor. 15:3)—The Savior's Work
Dead *to* Sin (Rom. 6:1)—The Christian's Position

58   The Joy of the Lord

In a Sinner's Salvation (Luke 15)
In a Saint's Preservation (Zeph. 3:17)
In a Disciple's Fruitfulness (John 15:24)
In His People's Presentation (Jude 24)

59   The Gospel Proclaims

Pardon for the Past (Isa. 55:7)
Power for the Present (2 Cor. 12:9)
Paradise for the Future (Luke 23:43)

1. Salvation from the Penalty of Sin
2. Deliverance from the Practice of Sin
3. Freedom from the Presence of Sin

60   The Sinner

Is described in God's Word as

A *rebel* needing Reconciliation (Rom. 5:10; Col. 1:21)
A *stranger* needing Regeneration (Eph. 2:12; John 3:7)
A *bond slave* needing Redemption (John 8:34; Eph. 1:7)

61 False Repentance

"I have sinned"—These words were uttered without repentance by

Pharaoh, the hardened sinner (Exod. 10:16)
Balaam, the religious money lover (Num. 22:34)
Achan, the covetous Israelite (Josh. 7:20)
Judas, the devil possessed traitor (Matt. 27:4)

Who all perished in their sin. Beacons, which may be used for the warning of others pursuing the same path.

62 True Repentance

"I have sinned"—These words were uttered sincerely by

David, convicted of his guilt (2 Sam. 12:13)
The Prodigal, convinced of his folly (Luke 15:18)
Sinners, confessing their need (Job 33:27)

Resulting in each case in forgiveness, reconciliation, and redemption. Such are the blessings of the saved sinner now (Eph. 1:7; Rom. 5:10).

63 Personal Questions

Where art thou? (Gen. 3:9)—To the Sinner hiding from God
What hast thou done? (Gen. 4:10)—To the Murderer of his Brother
What think ye of Christ? (Matt. 22:42)—To the Religious, but Unsaved Sinner

64 Fourfold View of a Sinner

Dead in Sin (Eph. 2:1)—Separated from God
Walking in Darkness (John 12:35)—Wandering from God
Living in Rebellion (Rom. 5:10)—At Enmity with God
Despising the Gospel (2 Thess. 2:8)—Fighting against God

65 Divine Love

Manifested, in the sending of Christ (1 John 4:9)
Commended, in the Death of Christ (Rom. 5:8)
Despised, in the rejection of Christ (2 Thess. 2:10)

66 Fourfold View of a Christian

A *Sinner* saved by Grace (1 Tim. 1:15; Eph. 2:8)
A *Son* born into God's Family (John 1:12; 1 John 3:2)
A *Saint* called to Holiness (Rom. 1:6; Eph. 5:3)
A *Servant* to work for Christ (John 12:26; Col. 3:24)

67 True Conversion

May be described as

Repentance toward God, in Mind (Acts 20:21)
Receiving from God, His Gift (John 1:12)
Returning to God, in Way (Ps. 119:59)
Relying on God, in Faith (2 Tim. 1:10)

68 Fourfold View of Christ

Son of God, Revealing the Father (John 1:18)
Son of Man, Seeking the Lost (Luke 19:10)
Sacrifice for Sin (1 Peter 3:18)
Savior of Sinners (1 Tim. 1:15)

69 Man in Four Conditions

Revealing his Creator—Likeness in *Innocency* (Gen. 1:26)
Ruined by Satan—Fallen under *Sin* (Rom. 5:12)
Redeemed by the Death of Christ—In *Grace* (Gal. 3:13)
Regenerated by the Holy Spirit—Through *Faith* (Titus 3:5)

70   Himself

The Person of Christ and His Work

"Himself took part of the same" (Heb. 2:14)—Incarnation
"He gave Himself for me" (Gal. 2:20)—Substitution
"By Himself purged our sins" (Heb. 1:3)—Purification
"To present to Himself the Church" (Eph. 5:27)—
  Glorification

71   Things Eternal

Eternal Redemption (Heb. 9:12)—Through Christ's
  Death
Eternal Salvation (Heb. 5:9)—By Christ's Power
Eternal Life (Rom. 6:3)—In Christ Risen
Eternal Glory (1 Peter 5:10)—Awaiting Christ's own

72   The Blood of Christ

What it does for all who believe

It is the Cause of Justification (Rom. 5:9)
It is the Ground of Peace (Col. 1:20)
It is the Price of Redemption (Eph. 1:7)
It is the Means of Sanctification (Heb. 10:10)
It is the Power for Victory (Rev. 12:11, 12)

73   Joy

Joy of Christ in Redemption (Matt. 13:20)
Joy in Heaven over Sinners Saved (Luke 15:7)
Joy on Earth by the Gospel (Acts 8:8)
Joy in the Heart (Rom. 20:13)—By Faith
Joy Unspeakable (1 Peter 1:8)—In Trial

74   To All

Love, the Attitude of God (John 3:16)—To All
Life, the Free Gift of God (Rom. 7:23)—For All
Liberty, Proclaimed in the Gospel (Acts 28:18)—Unto All

75   Things Worth Taking

Take the *water* of Life (Rev. 22:17)—For Salvation
Take hold of *instruction* (Prov. 4:13)—For Edification
Take Christ's *yoke* (Matt. 11:29)—In Submission
Take up the *cross* (Mark 8:34)—In Discipleship
Take the *armor* of God (Eph. 6:13)—In Defense

76   What the Blood of Christ Does

It has made Peace (Col. 1:20)
It has procured Redemption (Eph. 1:7)
It is the cause of Justification (Rom. 5:9)
It looses from Sin's Power (Rev. 1:7)
It cleanses from Sin's Pollution (1 John 1:7)
It gives entrance to God's presence (Heb. 10:19)

77   Christ Unchanging

Christ as *foundation* (1 Peter 2:6)—Can never be moved
Christ as *life* (Col. 3:4)—Can never be forfeited
Christ as *peace* (Eph. 2:14)—Can never be broken
Christ as *hope* (1 Tim. 1:1)—Can never be lost

78   Three Great Transitions

From Death to Life (John 5:24)
From Darkness to Light (1 Peter 2:9)
From Satan to God (Acts 26:18)

79   The Savior

A Savior Born (Luke 2:11)—Incarnation
A Savior Sent (John 3:17)—Salvation
A Savior Suffering (Matt. 27:42)—Substitution
A Savior Risen (Acts 13:23)—In Life
A Savior Exalted (Acts 5:31)—In Power
A Savior Coming (Phil. 3:20)—In Glory

80   All Nations

God will have all men to be Saved (1 Tim. 2:4)
The Ransom of Christ is for all (1 Tim. 2:6)
The Gospel is preached to all Nations (Matt. 28:19)
The Saved are from all Kingdoms (Rev. 7:9)

81   Work and Wages

Wages of Sin (Rom. 6:23)
Wages of Unrighteousness (2 Peter 2:15)
Wages of Christ Rejection (Rev. 20:12)
Wages of Faithful Service (John 4:36)

82   How the Lord Keeps

Those who put their trust in Him

As a Deposit in a Bank (2 Tim. 1:12)—Securely
As a Shepherd his Sheep (Jer. 31:10)—Faithfully
As a Watchman his Charge (Ps. 121:3)—Wakefully
As the Apple of the Eye (Deut. 32:10)—Tenderly

83   Three Titles of Christ

The Dayspring (Luke 1:78)—At Birth
The Daysman (Job 9:33)—In Death
The Day Star (2 Peter 1:19)—At His Advent

The *First* has reference to His coming in Grace.
The *Second* connects with His Sacrificial Death.
The *Third* points on to His coming in Glory.

84   Christ, Our Captain

The same word is rendered "Captain" (Heb. 2:10); "Prince" (Acts 3:15); "Author" (Heb. 12:2). He originates, works out, goes before, takes command, and leads on to victory.

His Infinite Wisdom (1 Cor. 1:24, 30)
His Unfailing Resources (Eph. 3:8)
His Supreme Authority (Matt. 28:18)
His Almighty Power (Heb. 1:3)
His Mighty Triumph (2 Cor. 2:14)
His Ultimate Victory (1 Cor. 15:57)

85   The Word of God

And its power in those who believe

As the Ingrafted Word received, it Saves (James 1:21)
As the Incorruptible Word believed, it Regenerates (1 Peter 1:21)
As the Cleansing Word submitted to, it Purifies (John 15:3)
As the Sanctifying Word obeyed, it Separates (John 17:17)

86   Sheep

Sheep going astray (Isa. 53:6)
Sheep sought and found (Luke 15:7, 10)
Sheep returned to the Shepherd (1 Peter 2:25)
Sheep in Green Pastures (Ps. 23:2)

87   The Sinner and the Savior

The sinner's need: the Savior's fulness

Hungry—Christ is Bread (John 6:33)
Thirsty—Christ is Drink (John 6:55)
Naked—Christ is Righteousness (Jer. 33:16)
Ignorant—Christ is Wisdom (1 Cor. 1:30)
Poor—Christ is Riches (Eph. 3:8)

88   Things Worth "Laying Up"

Treasures in Heaven (Matt. 6:20)

Word of God in the Heart (Job 22:22)
Goodness to them that fear God (Ps. 31:19)
Hope laid up in Heaven (Col. 1:5)
A Crown of Righteousness (2 Tim. 4:8)

89   Eternal Realities

Saved with an Eternal Salvation (Heb. 5:9)
Possessors of Eternal Life (1 John 5:8)
Passing on to an Eternal Inheritance (Heb. 9:15)
Called to an Eternal Glory (1 Peter 5:10)
Dwelling in an Eternal House (2 Cor. 5:1)

90   In Heaven

A Father in Heaven (Matt. 5:16)—By Regeneration
A Name written in Heaven (Luke 10:20)—By Grace
A Citizenship in Heaven (Phil. 3:20)—By Calling
An Inheritance in Heaven (1 Peter 1:4)—By Faith

BLACKBOARD TALKS

91   God's Way

WAY
of Salvation (Acts 16:17)
of Life (Jer. 21:8)
of Peace (Luke 1:79)

92   Four Gospel R's

R
uin—"Labor and heavy laden" (Matt. 11:28)
emedy—"I will give you rest" (Matt. 11:28)
eception—"Rest on Words" (2 Chr. 32:8)
ejection—"Ye will not come" (John 5:40)

93   Some Bible "Be's"

BE
ye reconciled (2 Cor. 5:20)—As Enemies
Ye saved (Isa. 45:22)—As Sinners
ye holy (1 Peter 1:15)—As Saints
ye ready (Matt. 24:44)—As Servants

94   Bible Books

BOOK of **L**
aw (Gal. 3:10)—brings the Curse
ife (Phil. 4:3)—Family Register
abor (Rev. 22:10)—of Reward

1. The Law condemns, but cannot give Life
2. God gives Life as a Free Gift
3. Grace rewards all true Labor for Christ

95   Christ, the Savior

Promised (Gen. 3:15)—in Eden
Provided (Luke 2:11)—at Bethlehem
Presented (Luke 2:22)—at Jerusalem
Preached (Acts 5:31)—to All Mankind

96   Right Ways

WAY *to* of of **H**eaven (Matt. 7:14)
appiness (Ps. 119:1)
oliness (Isa. 35:8)

97   Great Redemption

REDEEMED By Christ's Blood (1 Peter 1:19)
From all Iniquity (Titus 2:14)
Unto God (Rev. 5:9)

98   Jesus and the Children

(Mark 10:13-16)

Anxious Mothers, bringing Children *to* Jesus
Angry Disciples, sending away *from* Jesus
Alluring Savior, welcoming and blessing

99   Great Invitations

Come
Look
Turn
UNTO **M**E
(Matt. 11:28)—For Rest
(Isa. 45:22)—For Life
(Neh. 1:9)—For Restoration

100   Christ, the Shepherd

ood
reat
lorious
G **S**HEPHERD
(John 10:11) Died
(Heb. 13:20) Lives
(1 Peter 5:4) Comes

101   Peace

P**EACE** P*rocured* at the Cross (Col. 1:20)
roclaimed in the Gospel (Acts 10:36)
ossessed by Faith (Rom. 5:1)

102   Life

F*orfeited* by Sin (Rom. 5:12)
ound in Christ (1 John 5:11)
ree Gift of God (Rom. 6:23)

103   The Lost Sheep

S*traying*   S*heep* (Luke 15:4)—Sinner
eeking   *hepherd* (Luke 15:4)—Savior
upported   *aved* (Luke 15:5)—Saint

104   New Things

A N**EW** Covenant by Redemption (Heb. 11:15)
Creature by Regeneration (2 Cor. 5:17)
Song in Resurrection Life (Ps. 40:13)
Walk in Righteousness (Ps 23:4)

105   Children

C**HILDREN** By Christ's Blood (1 Peter 1:19)
From all Iniquity (Titus 2:14)
Unto God (Rev. 5:9)

106   The Love of God

U*ndeserved* (1 John 4:10)
nasked (Rom. 5:8)
nending (Jer. 31:3)

107   **Savior**

A   (Luke 2:11)—Provided
Thy **S**AVIOR   (John 4:42)—Presented
My   (Luke 1:47)—Possessed

108   **The Lost Silver**

Lost in the House—The Sinner Dead, Helpless
ighted Candle—The Word used by the Spirit
ooked for Diligently—The Soul-winner's Work
abor Rewarded—Found, Converted, Restored

109   **Great Truths**

Regeneration by the Spirit (John 3:5)
esurrection by the Lord (Rom. 4:4)
estoration to the Father (Luke 15:24)

1. New Birth—the beginning of Christian Life
2. New Walk—the evidence of having New Life
3. Relation and Communion—the result of Conversion

110   **The Bible**

Lamp of Life (Ps. 119:150)—To Guide
ighthouse of Truth (Ps. 19:11)—To Warn
etter of Grace (Luke 14:17)—To Invite
ibrary of Wisdom (2 Tim. 3:16)—To Enlighten

111   **God's Great Things**

                        Sin of Man (Gen. 6:5)
GREAT **G** *alvation* of God (Heb. 2:3)
race on Believers (Acts 4:33)
ulf fixed (Luke 24:26)

112   Great Gospel Truths

Ruin by Sin (Rom. 5:7)
edemption by Blood (Eph. 1:7)
eception by Faith (John 1:12)

113   From Condemnation to Liberty

Sin's Wages (Rom. 6:23)—The Sinner's Due
atan's Power (Heb. 2:18)—Sinner's Slavery
avior's Triumph (Heb. 2:14)—The Cross
inner's Deliverance (Col. 1:13)—Conversion

114   Children

Saved   **C**HILDREN   come to Jesus
Singing   commended by Jesus
Scoffing   condemned to judgment

Matt. 19:14; Matt. 21:15; 2 Kings 2:24

115   Bible Birds

A BIRD
Sacrificed (Lev. 14:4)
Sent Forth (Gen. 8:9)
Spreading Wings (Deut. 32:11)

1. Type of Christ's Sacrifice—for Pardon
2. Emblem of Resurrection—for Peace
3. Symbol of Salvation—for Power

116   Mounts of Scripture

MOUNT
of Substitution (Gen. 22:1-14)
of Instruction (Matt. 5:1)
of Transfiguration (Matt. 17:1)

1. The Sinner's Salvation—Procured
2. The Disciple's Instruction—Provided
3. The Glory to be Revealed—Prefigured

117   **Bible Doors**

An Open   **D**OOR   (John 10:9)—To Enter
A Closed   (Rev. 3:20)—To Open
A Shut   (Luke 13:25)—To Exclude

   1. Christ the Only Way to God—Door of Salvation
   2. Christ seeks an Entrance—Door of Acceptance
   3. Christ rises for Judgment—Door of Mercy closed

118   **Scripture Banners**

Gospel   **B**ANNER   of Love (Sol. 2:5)
Christian's   of Truth (Ps. 20:5)
Warrior's   of Victory (Exod. 17:5)

   1. Under Love's Banner, Confiding—the Believing Sinner is *Safe*
   2. Holding forth God's Truth—The Christian is *Strong*
   3. Fighting behind Jehovah's Name—The Victory is *Sure*

119   **Honey Lesssons**

HONEY   in the Flower (Jer. 41:8)
        in the Comb (Prov. 16:24)
        in the Mouth (Ezek. 3:3)

   1. Like the Gospel *Promised*
   2. Like the Gospel *Proclaimed*
   3. Like the Gospel *Posessed*

120   **Darkness and Light**

DARKNESS   of Sin (Ps. 107:10)
          of the Savior (Mark 15:33)
          The Deliverance (1 Peter 2:9)
          The Sinner' Doom (Jude 13)

   1. The State of all by Nature (Eph. 5:8)
   2. The Sign of Sin's Judgment (Lude 23:45)
   3. The Great Transition (Col. 1:13)
   4. The Galling Chains (2 Peter 2)

121   Christer, Our Rock

R
OCK
   of Song (Isa. 92:11)
of Salvation (2 Sam. 22:47)
of Shelter (Isa. 32:2)
of Stability (Ps. 40:2)

122   Christ's Ability

A
BLE
   to Save (Heb. 7:25)
to Succor (Heb.2:18)
to Subdue (Phil.3:21)

1. He Saves Sinners (1 Tim. 1:15)
2. He Succors His own (2 Cor. 6:2)
3. He Subdues all (1 Cor. 15:28)

123   Three "Musts" for Sinners

We   **M**UST   Die (2 Sam. 14:14)
Ye   be Born Again (John 3:7)
We   be Saved (Acts 4:12)

1. The Result of Adam's Sin (Rom. 5:12)
2. Because of our Condition by Nature (Eph. 2:1)
3. By Faith in Christ's Person and Work (Acts 14:31)

124   The Savior's "Musts"

He   **M**UST   be "Lifted up" in Death (John 3:14)
He   be "Raised" to Life (Matt. 16:21)
He   Reign in Glory (1 Cor. 15:25)

125   Our Names

S
inners by Nature (Rom. 5:19)
ons by New Birth (John 1:12-14)
ervants by Calling (Gal 1:5)
trangers in Conduct (1 Peter 2:11)

126   Christ's Coming

in Judgment upon Sinners will be

Swift as the Lightning (Matt. 24:27)
udden as the Flood (Matt. 24:39)
ure as the Word (Matt. 24:35)
ecret as the Thief (Matt. 24:27)

127   Divers Ways

WAY
of Death (Prov. 19:12)
of Life (Jer. 21:8)
of Holiness (Isa. 35:8)
of Happiness (Prov. 3:17)

128   Three States of Soul

Sin of the   **S**OUL   (Ezek. 18:20)
alvation of the   (1 Peter 1:9)
atisfaction of the   (Isa. 58:5)

129   Sin

SIN
Committed (1 John 3:8)
Concealed (Prov. 33:13)
Confessed (1 John 1:9)
Cancelled (Ps. 32:2)

130   The Love of God

UN
deserved (1 John 4:10)
asked (Rom. 5:8)
measured (Eph. 2:4)
reserved (John 3:16)
appropriated (2 Thess. 2:16)

EMBLEMATIC
GOSPEL SUBJECTS

These subjects may be illustrated by using the objects and emblems peculiar to each, or by drawing on the blackboard simple outlines suited to the message.

131   Flowers and Their Messages

Wild Flowers—Man in Nature (Ps. 103:15)
Sweet Flowers—An Emblem of Christ (Song 5:13)
Spring Flowers—New Life in the Soul (Song 2:12)
Fading Flowers—Brevity of Life (1 Peter 1:24)

132   Trusters in Christ

As Conies in the Rock (Ps. 104:18)—Hiding in Christ
As Dove in the Ark (Gen. 8:9)—Resting on Christ
As Spider in the Palace (Prov. 30:28)—Clinging to Christ

133   Four Hearts

A Deceitful Heart (Jer. 17:9)—To Depart from God
A Believing Heart (Rom. 10:9)—To Trust in God
A Purified Heart (Acts 15:9)—To Love God
A True Heart (Heb. 10:22)—To Worship God

134   Scripture Nails

Nail of Justice (Judg. 5:26)—Brings Death
Nails of Sacrifice (John 20:25)—Procures Life
Nail of Suretyship (Col. 2:14)—Proclaims Forgiveness
Nail of Power (Isa. 22:23)—Gives Assurance

135 Emblems of Faith

Faith's *Heart* trusts Christ's Work (Isa. 53:5)
Faith's *Ear* hears Christ's Words (John 5:24)
Faith's *Eye* sees Christ's Person (John 1:36)
Faith's *Hand* receives Christ's Gifts (John 17:8)

136 What the Sinner Is Like

A Wild Colt (Job 11:12)—State by Birth
A Black Ethiopian (Jer. 13:23)—Condition by Nature
A Spotted Leopard (Jer. 13:23)—Cannot be altered
A Named Sheep (John 10:27)—Saved by Grace

137 Emblems of the Savior

A *Lamb* Without Blemish (1 Peter 1:19)—Our Sacrifice
　　In Nature and Position before God

A *Bird* Alive and Clean (Lev. 14:4)—Our Substitute
　　In Life and Character before Men

A *Goat* bearing a Burden (Lev. 16:22)—Our Sin-bearer
　　In death, in His People's stead

138 Lesson on Leaves

Fading Leaves (Isa. 64:6)—Life's Brevity
Falling Leaves (Dan. 4:12)—Death's Approach
Driven Leaves (Job 13:21)—Divine Retribution
Healing Leaves (Rev. 22:2)—Christ's Power
Evergreen Leaves (Ps. 1:3)—A Healthy Christian

139 Bible Stars

Star of Promise (Num. 24:17)—Speaks of Christ
Star of Guidance (Matt. 2:10)—Leads to Christ
Stars of Testimony (Rev. 1:20)—Shining for Christ
Stars of Brightness (Dan. 12:3)—Glory with Christ
Stars of Wandering (Jude 13)—Severed from Christ

140   Bible Gates

A Strait Gate (Matt. 7:13)—For Life
A Gate of Righteousness (Ps. 118:19)—For Pardon
A Gate of Thanksgiving (Ps. 100:4)—For Praise
A Gate of Pearl (Rev. 21:21)—For Glory

141   Bible Doors

A Sin-stained Door (Gen. 4:7)—For Guilt
An Opened Door (Acts 14:27)—For Testimony
A Blood Sprinkled Door (Exod. 12:22)—For Safety
A Divinely Shut Door (Gen. 7:16)—For Security

142   Scripture Seals

Sin Sealed for Judgment (Job 14:17)
Savior Sealed for Service (John 6:27)
Sinner sets his Seal to God's Word (John 3:33)
Saint Sealed for Glory (Eph. 4:30)

143   Snow Lessons

Snow White Leper (2 Kings 5:27)—The Sinner's State
Snow Water cannot Cleanse (Job 9:30)—Man's Efforts Vain
Whiter than Snow (Ps. 51:7)—Power of Christ's Blood
Purer than Snow (Lam. 4:7)—Separated to God

144   Worms

The Sinner, Fallen and Helpless (Job 25:6)
The Savior, Lowly and Suffering (Ps. 22:6)
The Saved One, Used by God (Isa. 41:41)
The Scorner, Smitten by Judgment (Acts 12:23)

145   Trees and Their Messages

A Corrupt Tree (Matt. 7:17)—Sin in Nature
A Barren Tree (Matt. 21:19)—Empty Profession
A Condemned Tree (Luke 13:6)—Lost Opportunities
A Fruitful Tree (Ps. 1:3)—Abiding in Grace

146   Bible Lamps

An Empty Lamp (Matt. 25:8)—Of Profession
A Well-filled Lamp (Matt. 25:7)—Of Possession
A Burning Lamp (Ps. 119:105)—The Word
A Well-trimmed Lamp (Exod. 27:25)—The Christian
A Lamp put out (Prov. 13:9)—The Ungodly

147   The Sower and His Seed

The Sower, Christ and His Servants (Mark 4:14)
The Seed, the Word of God (Luke 8:11)
The Soils, Hearts of Men (Matt. 13:19, 23)
"The Sequel, Stolen by Satan" (v. 19)
"Withered by trial" (v. 21)
"Checked by Worldliness" (v. 22)
"Fruitage by Faith" (v. 23)

148   A Sparrow Lesson

Worthless in Value (Matt. 10:29)
Cared for by God (Luke 12:6)
Redeemed and Liberated (Lev. 14:4, 6)
A Home in God's Temple (Ps. 84:3)

Emblematic of the sinner in nature, redeemed, liberated, resting in
Christ, and at home with God.

149   The Swallow

A Restless Bird, like the Sinner (Isa. 57:20)
A Mourning Bird, like the Sad (Isa. 38:14)
A Redeemed Bird, resting in Altars (Ps. 84:3)
A Migrating Bird, leaving for other Climes (Phil. 1:23)

150   The Dove

A Restless Dove in a doomed World (Gen. 8:8)
A Sheltered Dove in the Ark (Gen. 8:11)
A Dove in the Cleft of a Rock (Jer. 48:28)
A Dove Fleeing Away (Ps. 55:6)

Emblematic of the soul in the world, in Christ, in safety, in Heaven.

151   Bible Hills

Sinai, the Law (Exod. 20)—Conviction
Ebal, the Curse (Deut. 11)—Condemnation
Moriah, the Altar (Gen. 22)—Substitution
Zion, the Blessing (Ps. 133)—Life
Olivet, the Kingdom (Zech. 14)—Glory

152   Bundles

Bundle of Sticks (Acts 27:3)—Death by Sin
Bundle of Life (1 Sam. 25:29)—Life in Christ
Bundle of Myrrh (Song 1:13)—Communion
Bundle of Tares (Matt. 13:30)—Judgment

153   Steps on Faith's Ladder

Object: A ladder of five steps, each of different color

No Faith (Mark 4:40)
Little Faith (Matt. 6:30)
Great Faith (Matt. 8:10)
Strong in Faith (Rom. 4:20)
Full of Faith (Acts 6:5)

154   Christ for Me

On His Shoulder (Luke 15:5)—Rescued
In His Hand (John 10:27)—Secure
At His Feet (Luke 10:39)—Learning
On His Bosom (John 13:23)—Communing

155   Links in Love's Chain

Object: A chain of varied colored links, with these words on each, may
be used for an object lesson

No Love (John 5:40)
Little Love (Luke 7:47)
Much Love (Luke 8:47)
Abundant Love (2 Cor. 12:15)
Fervent Love (1 Peter 1:22)

156   A Rainbow Lesson

As seen by Noah, Sign of God's Covenant in Grace
As seen by Ezekiel, Pledge of God's Faithfulness, in
Government
As seen by John, Seal of God's Promise, in Glory

The "Bow" in the Cloud tells of Judgment past
The "Bow" in the Heavens, of continued Mercy
The "Bow" around the Throne, of endless Glory

157   Night Scenes

A Night Visitor, in Soul Anxiety (John 3:1)
A Night of Awakening and Conversion (Acts 16:25, 34)
A Night of Betrayal and Remorse (John 13:20)
A Night of Arousing and Alarm (Matt. 25:6)

158   A Color Lesson

Blacker than Coal (Lam. 4:8)—A Sinner by Nature
Whiter than Snow (Ps. 51:7)—Cleansed by Blood
Brighter than the Stars (Dan. 12:3)—In Glory

159 Noble Trees

Emblems of True Christian Life

The Goodly *Cedar,* deeply rooted, long lived (Ps. 104:16)
The Upright *Palm,* lofty, stately, green (Ps. 92:12)
The Green *Olive,* ever fresh, yielding oil (Ps. 52:8)
The Fruitful *Vine,* planted, pruned, profitable (John 15:11)

160 Stages in Grace

Which the soul may experience

Grace Received (2 Cor. 6:1)—In Salvation
Abundant Grace (Rom. 5:17)—For Life
Great Grace (Acts 4:33)—In Testimony
More Grace (James 4:6)—In Trial
All Grace (2 Cor. 9:8)—For everything

161 Heart Conditions

Hard Heart of Unbelief (Mark 8:17)
Opened Heart, in Anxiety (Acts 16:14)
Broken Heart, by Contrition (Ps. 51:17)
Purposed Heart, to Cleave (Acts 11:23)

162 Seats of Scripture

Seat of Moses (Matt. 23:2)—Law
Seat of Mercy (Exod. 25:21, 22)—Grace
Seat of Majesty (Heb. 8:2)—Glory
Seat of Judgment (2 Cor. 5:10)—Reward

163 Conies

Unclean by Nature (Lev. 11:5)
Feeble in State (Prov. 30:26)
Secure in Rock (Ps. 104:18)

In these three particulars they represent the sinner
  1. In Guilt (Isa. 64:6)
  2. In Weakness (Rom. 5:6)
  3. In Christ (Ps. 94:22)

PICTURES FROM THE PATRIARCHS

164   Adam, the First Man

Read Genesis 2, 3; Romans 5:12-18

Formed in God's Image (Gen. 1:26)—Innocent
Fell by Disobedience (Gen. 3:6)—Ruined
Forbidden to eat of Tree (Gen. 2:17)—Tried
Forfeited Life and Place (Gen. 3:24)—Expelled

165   The Promised Deliverer

(Genesis 3:15; Luke 2:11; Galatians 4:4)

Seed of the Woman—Christ as Man
Son of God—Christ as Divine
Satan's Overcomer—Christ as Victor
Savior of Sinners—Christ as Deliverer

166   The Home in Eden

(Genesis 2:6-15; Revelation 22:1-14)

Prepared by God (Gen. 2:8; Heb. 11:16)
Provided for Man (Gen. 2:8; John 14:2)
Place of Delight (Gen. 2:8; Ps. 16:11)
Promise to Overcomer (Gen. 2:9; Rev. 2:7)

> Justice, excluded fallen man from Eden
> Grace, admits saved man to Heaven
> Glory, is secured for ever, in Christ

167   Aprons and Coats

(Genesis 3:7-21; Philippians 3:9; 2 Corinthians 5:21)

Afraid of God—The Sinner's Dread
Hiding from Him—A False Refuge
Fig Leaf Aprons—Man's own Work
Coats of Skin—Sacrifice and Salvation
Covered and Accepted—Imputed Righteousness

168   Cain, the First Formalist

(Genesis 4:1-16; 1 John 3:12; Jude 11)

Born, a Fallen Sinner—His Ruin
Brought a Bloodless Offering—His Religion
Disowned his State—His Pride
Denied the Atonement—His Unbelief
Angry at God's Approval—His Envy
Slays his Brother—His Crime
Despises God's Offered Mercy—His Choice
Goes out from God's Presence—His End

169   Abel, the First Martyr

(Genesis 4:1-8; Hebrews 11:4; 12:24; John 3:12)

A Confessed Sinner (Job 40:4)
A Believing Offerer (Isa. 53:5)
Accepted in his Substitute (Eph. 1:6)
A Justified Man (Acts 13:39)
A Suffering Saint (1 Peter 2:21)

170   Enoch, Who Did Not Die

(Genesis 5:21-24; Hebrews 11:5; Jude 14)

The Times he lived in (Heb. 6:5, with 2 Peter 3:3, 4)
Date of his Conversion (Heb. 5:22, with John 3:7)
His Walk with God (Heb. 5:24, with 1 John 1:7)
His Testimony for God (Jude 14, with John 15:27)
His Translation to God (Gen. 5:23, with 1 Thess. 4:17)

171   The Old World's Wickedness

(Genesis 6:1-13; Luke 17:26; 2 Peter 3:5-6)

Great Men of Renown (2 Tim. 3:2)
Great Sinners before God (Jer. 2:22)
Disregarded God's Claim (Ps. 73:8)
Disbelieved God's Judgment (2 Peter 3:4)
Their Folly was great (Matt. 24:38)
The Doom was Sudden (Matt. 24:39)

172   **The Ark of Safety**

(Genesis 6, 7 and 8)

The Place of Safety—"Make thee an Ark" (Gen. 6:14)
The Divine Invitation—"Come" (Gen. 7:1)
The Ready Response—"They went in" (Gen. 7:15)
The Great Security—"The Lord shut him in" (Gen. 7:16)
The Call to Liberty—"Go forth" (Gen. 8:16)

173   **The Rainbow, the Covenant,
and the Promise**

(Genesis 9:8-17; Isaiah 54:9)

The Covenant of God (Gen. 9:9)—In Grace
The Sign thereof (Gen. 9:13)—The Bow
The Seal of it (Gen. 9:15)—His Word

174   **Abram, the Pilgrim**

(Genesis 12:1; Hebrews 11:8)

The Lord's Call (Gen. 12:1)—The Gospel
Faith's Response (Gen. 12:4)—Conversion
The Promised Presence (Gen. 12:7)—Blessing
The First Difficulty (Gen. 12:10)—Trial

175   **Sodom and its Doom**

(Genesis 18:20; 19:17-25; Luke 17:29)

The Doomed City—Type of the World (Gen. 18:20)
The Earnest Intercessor—Abraham prayed (Gen. 18:23)
The Divine Deliverance—"Bring them out" (Gen. 19:12)
The Way of Escape—"Escape for thy Life" (Gen. 19:17)
The Procrastinator—Lot's Wife (Gen. 19:26)
The Place of Safety—Zoar (Gen. 19:23)

176 The Sacrifice on Moriah

(Genesis 22:1-14; Hebrews 11:17)

The Father who gave (John 3:16)
The Obedient Son who yielded (Isa. 53:7)
The Altar on the Hill (Luke 23:33)
The Uplifted Knife (Zech. 13:7)
The Cords Unloosed (Acts 2:24)
The Only Begotten Raised (Heb. 11:19)
Return to the Father's House (John 14:2)

177 The Winning of the Bride

(Genesis 24; Matthew 22:1; Acts 15:14; 1 Peter 1:12)

The Father and Son in Hebron (Gen. 24:1, 6)—Heaven
The Servant sent Forth (Gen. 24:10, 12)—The Spirit's Work
The Bride is met (Gen. 24:15, 22)—The Sinner Attracted
The Message is told (Gen. 24:35, 38)—The Gospel Message
The Jewels and Raiment (Gen. 24:53)—The Gospel's
    Blessing
The Great Decision (Gen. 24:58)—The Heart Won
The Homeward Journey (Gen. 24:60, 61)—From Cross to
    Glory
The Meeting (Gen. 24:68, 69)—The Second Advent

178 Joseph, Like Jesus

(Genesis 37-41; Psalm 105:17)

The Son of his Father's Love (Gen. 37:3; John 3:35)
The Object of his Brother's Hatred (Gen. 37:4; John 15:23)
Rejected and Sold (Gen. 37:28; Matt. 27:28)
Accused and Condemned (Gen. 39:19; Mark 14:56)
Numbered with Transgressors (Gen. 39:20; Luke 23:39, 41)
Exalted and Honored (Gen. 41:43; Phil. 2:9, 10)
Savior and Lord (Gen. 41:46; Acts 2:36; 4:12)

TEACHINGS FROM THE TYPES

179   The Babe in the Bulrushes

(Exodus 2:1-10; Hebrews 11:23; Acts 7:20)

A Cruel Edict (Exod. 1:22)—The Sentence of Death
(Heb. 2:14)
A Beautiful Child (Acts 7:20)—An Object of Love
(John 3:16)
A Way of Escape (Exod. 2:3)—Through Death (Ps. 18:16)
A Royal Rescue (Exod. 2:5)—To Life and Glory (2 Tim. 2:10)

180   Slavery in Egypt

(Exodus 1:11-13; 5:6, 23; John 8:34)

Pharaoh a Tyrant—Like Satan
Israelites his Slaves—Like Sinners
Unable to free themselves—"Without Strength"
The Seven "I wills"—"God, our Savior"
Complete Deliverance (Deut. 5:15)—"Great Salvation"

181   Egypt's First-born Slain

(Exodus 11:1; 12:12-29; Psalm 78:51)

The Divine Judgment (Exod. 11:12)—The Wages of Sin
All shared it alike (Exod. 11:29)—No Difference
It was sudden (Exod. 11:30)—Like the Judgment
At an unexpected hour (Exod. 11:29)—"When ye think not"

182   The Passover and Its Lessons

(Exodus 12:1-13; 1 Corinthians 5:7)

The Lamb Chosen (Exod. 12:2)—Christ (1 Peter 1:20)
The Lamb Kept (Exod. 12:5)—Christ in Life (Matt. 3:17)
The Lamb Slain (Exod. 12:6)—Christ's Death (1 Peter 1:19)
The Blood Sprinkled (Exod. 12:7)—Faith's Appropriation
The Assurance Given (Exod. 12:23)—The Word of God

183   The Redeemed of the Lord

(Exodus 12:13-51; Psalm 103:1, 4; 107:1, 6)

A Saved People (Exod. 12:13, with Rom. 8:1)
A Satisfied People (Exod. 12:8, with John 6:53)
A Separated People (Exod. 12:31, with Gal. 1:4)
A Sanctified people (Exod. 13:1, with 1 Cor. 1:2)

184   The Passage of the Red Sea

(Exodus 14:1-31)

The Enemy Pursuing (Exod. 14:9)—Satan's Power
(Acts 26:18)
The People in Fear (Exod. 14:10)—Human Helplessness
(Ps. 116:1, 3)
God comes Between (Exod. 14:19)—God for us (Rom. 8:31)
The Sea Parted (Exod. 14:21)—Death Abolished (Heb. 2:14)
The Work of Faith (Exod. 14:22)—Faith's Acceptance
(Heb. 11:29)
The Resurrection Side (Exod. 14:31)—From Death to
Life (John 5:24)

185   Salvation and Its Song

(Exodus 14:13-30; 15:1-3)

Salvation all of God (Exod. 14:13, 14, with Jonah 2:9)
Salvation all for Man (Exod. 14:30, with Acts 16:31)
Salvation Seen and Known (Exod. 14:31, with Luke 2:30)
Salvation's Song of Triumph (Exod. 15:1, with Ps. 40:3)

186   Daily Bread in the Desert

(Exodus 16:1-11; Deuteronomy 8:3; Psalm 78:24)

The Free Gift of God (John 3:16; 6:51)
Sent down from Heaven (John 6:32)
Gathered or Trodden (John 1:12; Heb. 10:29)
White and Sweet (Ps. 19:10)

187   Streams in the Wilderness

(Exodus 17:1-7; Psalm 114:8; 1 Corinthians 10:4)

The Rock Smitten—Christ's Death (Isa. 53:4)
The Water Flowed—Life through Him (John 10:10)
The Great Invitation—"Come," "Take" (Isa. 55:1; Rev.
  22:17)

188   The First Battle

(Exodus 17:9-16; Deuteronomy 25:17)

The Enemy, a Kinsman—Like the Flesh (Gal. 5:17)
A Deceitful Attack—"The Hindmost," Backsliders
A Great Intercessor—Christ Above (Rom. 8:34)
A Sharp Sword—The Word of God (Heb. 4:12)
No Armistice—"No Confidence" (Phil. 3:2)

189   The Law From Sinai

(Exodus 20:1-21; Romans 5:20; Galatians 3:10)

The Ten Great Words—Jehovah's Demands
The Rash Promise—"We will do" (Exod. 19:8)
The Broken Vow—"Guilty of all" (James 2:10)
The Curse Earned—"Under the Curse" (Gal. 3:10)
The Altar of Stone (Exod. 20:25)—Redemption by Blood
  (Gal. 3:13)

190   The Hebrew Servant's Love

(Exodus 21:1-6; Ephesians 5:25-26; Galatians 2:20)

The Service of Freedom (Exod. 21:3)—Christ's (John 10:18)
The Service of Love (Exod. 21:5)—Christ's Surrender
(Eph. 5:2)
The Service of Sacrifice (Exod. 21:6)—Christ's
Substitution (Isa. 51:11)
The Service of Devotion (Exod. 21:6)—Christ's
Perpetual Service (Heb. 8:2)

191   The Beautiful Tabernacle

(Exodus 25, 26, with Hebrews 9:1)

A House for God (Exod. 25:8)—His Dwelling Place on
Earth (1 Cor. 3:16)
His People's Gifts (Exod. 25:1)—First Receivers, then
Givers (2 Cor. 9:8, 15)
His own Pattern (Exod. 25:9)—To be carefully Observed
(1 Cor. 3:10)
His Chosen Workmen (Exod. 31:1, 3)—Called and
Fitted (Eph. 4:11)
Furnished and Filled (Exod. 40:34)—Stablished,
Glorified (1 Peter 5:10)

192   The Gate of the Court

(Exodus 27:16; John 10:9)

Only one Entrance—"The Gate" (John 14:6)
Low and Wide—For "Whosoever" (John 3:16)
In the East—In the Light (John 3:19)
Easily Perceived—None other Name (Acts 4:12)
One Step In—"Out" or "In" (Eph. 2:12, 13)

193   The Altar and the Sacrifice

(Exodus 27:1; Leviticus 4:7, 29-33)

The Place of Sacrifice—The Cross of Christ
The Fire Ever Burning—Divine Justice
The Victim was Slain—Christ's Death
Hand on the Offering—Identification by Faith
The Blood was Shed—Christ's Atonement
The Sinner was Forgiven—Justified from All

194   The Ransom Money

(Exodus 30:11-12; 1 Peter 1:18-19; 1 Timothy 2:6)

A Ransom Needed (Psalm 49:7)
A Ransom Provided (Job 33:24)
A Ransom Accepted (Matt. 20:28)
A Ransom Rejected (Job 36:18)

195   The Laver and Its Water

(Exodus 30:17-21; Ephesians 5:26; Titus 3:5)

Its Place, before the Door—No Entrance Apart (John 3:5)
Its Use, to wash thereat—Washing of Regeneration
    (Titus 3:5)
Priests Washed Once—Symbol of new Birth (John 15:3)
Priests Wash Daily—Daily use of Word (Ps. 119:9)

196   The Leper, His Place and Cry

(Leviticus 13:1-18; Isaiah 6:5)

A Type of the Sinner, unclean and afar off

Leprosy, Sin in the Flesh—Man in Nature
The Leper's Place—"Without" (Eph. 2:12)
The Leper's State—Clothes Rent (Joel 2:13)
The Leper's Cry—"Unclean" (Isa. 64:6)

197   The Leper's Cleansing

(Leviticus 14:1-18; Luke 17:11-19)

The Priest Goes Forth—Christ Jesus Came (1 Tim. 1:15)
A Sacrifice Provided—Christ gave Himself (1 Tim. 2:6)
Living Bird let Loose—Christ Raised (Rom. 4:25)
Water Sprinkled—The Word Received (1 Peter 1:23)
Pronounced Clean—"Ye are Washed" (1 Cor. 6:11)
Set Apart and Anointed—The Spirit Given (2 Cor. 1:21)
A True Worshiper—Gives Thanks (Luke 17:17)

198   The Scapegoat and His Burden

(Leviticus 16:1-9; Isaiah 53:6; Hebrews 9:27-28)

The Two Goats represent Christ as the One Sacrifice

The Goat Slain—Christ's Atonement, Godward
The Living Goat—Christ's Sin-bearing, Manward
The Sins Confessed—Laid upon Christ (Isa. 53:6)
Sins Borne Away—Put away by Him (Heb. 9:21)
Never to Return—Sins Forgotten (Heb. 10:17)

199   The Grapes of Eshcol

(Numbers 13:17-24; Ephesians 1:13)

Canaan, a Type of Heaven—Place of Blessing (Eph. 1:3)
Cluster of Grapes—Earnest of the Inheritance (Eph. 1:13)
Borne across Jordan—Heavenly things on Earth (Col. 3:1)
Living Witnesses—Christian Testimony (2 Tim. 1:12)

200 The Story of the Brazen Serpent

(Numbers 21:4-9; John 3:14-15)

Bitten Israelites—Sinners in the World (Rom. 5:12, 14)
Dying and Helpless—Man's Help Vain (Ps. 60:11)
A True Confession—"We have Sinned" (Job. 33:27)
A Divine Remedy—A Serpent on a Pole (John 3:14)
A Simple Way—Look and Live (Isa. 45:22)
A Sure Result—"He shall Live" (John 3:36)

201 Crossing the Jordan

(Joshua 3, 4; Psalm 114:3; Jeremiah 12:5)

The Swollen River—Death and Judgment
The Ark Enters—Christ in Death and Resurrection
The Waters Cut Off—Christ Abolished Death (1 Tim. 1:10)
The Redeemed Pass Over—Through Death to Life
  (Rom. 6:5, 6)
Stones set up in Canaan—Believer's "in Christ" (Eph. 2:6)

202 The House With the Scarlet Line

(Joshua 2:1; 6:17-25; Hebrews 11:31)

A City under Sentence—The World (Rom. 3:19)
A Sinner without Character—Rahab (1 Tim. 1:15)
A Message of Mercy—The Gospel (John 3:16)
A Confession of Fear—Convicted Sinner (Acts 16:30)
A True Token—The Blood of Christ (1 Peter 1:19)
A Sure Promise—The Word of God (John 10:28)

203   Achan, the Deceiver

(Joshua 7:1-26)

Sin Committed Secretly (Josh. 7:1)—The Guilt
Sin Sought out Searchingly (Josh. 7:22)—The Judgment
Sin Punished Surely (Josh. 7:24)—The Doom

204   Gideon, the Brave Soldier

(Judges 7:11-40)

A Meeting with God (Judg. 7:23)—Right with God
A Testimony at Home (Judg. 7:26)—Begins to Witness
A Testing for Service (Judg. 7:3, 6)—Learns God's Way
A Great Victory (Judg. 7:14)—Proves God's Power

205   Biographies in Ruth

(Ruth 1-4)

Naomi, the Backslider, Wandering and Restored
Orpah, the Worldling, Awakened, Halting, Turned Back
Ruth, the Believer, Decided, Confessing, in Christ
Boaz, Type of Christ, as Redeemer and Friend

KEY NOTES FROM THE TYPES

206 Samuel, the Boy Prophet

(1 Samuel 3:1-12)

Asked of God, in Prayer (1 Sam. 1:20)
Dedicated to God, in Faith (1 Sam. 1:28)
Called by God, in Grace (1 Samuel 2:4)
Approved of God, in Service (1 Sam. 2:19)

> The history of a true servant: saved, set apart, schooled, and successful.

207 David, the Shepherd Lad

(1 Samuel 16:1-13; 17:24-36)

A Beautiful Boy (1 Sam. 16:12)
A Keeper of Sheep (1 Sam. 16:11)
A Noble Deliverer (1 Sam. 17:34, 36)
A Skilled Musician (1 Sam. 16:18)
A Royal Servant (1 Sam. 16:21)

208 David, the Victor

(1 Samuel 17:1-52)

Anointed in Secret (1 Sam. 16:13)—His Call
Trained for Service (Ps. 77:70, 72)—His School
His Faith in God (1 Sam. 17:37)—His Fitness
His Fearless Confession (1 Sam. 17:45)—His Valor
His Sling and Stone (1 Sam. 17:40, 49)—His Weapons
His Complete Triumph (1 Sam. 17:50, 51)—His Victory

> Type of Christ's victory over Satan (Hebrews 2:14) and deliverance of His people (Colossians 1:13)

209 David and Jonathan

(1 Samuel 18:1-5; 19:1-7)

David, the Victor, seen and heard (1 Sam. 18:1)—Christ in Resurrection

Jonathan becomes his Friend (1 Sam. 18:1)—The Heart Won

Surrenders all to him (1 Sam. 18:2)—Devotion to Christ

Speaks well of David (1 Sam. 18:4)—True Testimony

Delighted much in David (1 Sam. 19:2)—Communion with Christ

Persecuted for David's Sake (1 Sam. 20:33)—Suffering for Christ

210 Mephibosheth, the Lame Prince

(2 Samuel 9:1-13)

Belonged to a Ruined House (2 Sam. 9:3)—Like Sinners (Rom. 5:12)

Personally Lame and Helpless (2 Samuel 9:3)—Without Strength (Rom. 5:8)

Position, Afar off (2 Sam. 9:4)—Afar off (Eph. 2:12)

A Subject of Divine Grace (2 Sam. 9:3)—God's Kindness (Titus 3:4)

Brought Near by Another (2 Sam. 9:5)—Made Nigh (Eph. 2:13)

Confesses his State (2 Sam. 9:8)—Chief of Sinners (1 Tim. 1:15)

Is Welcomed in Grace (2 Sam. 9:10)—Reconciled (Rom. 5:10)

Set in a Royal Position (2 Sam. 9:10)—Sons (1 John 3:1)

Receive a Kingly Portion (2 Sam. 9:13)—As He is (1 John 4:17)

211   Absalom, the Rebel

(2 Samuel 13:28; 14:24)

A Guilty Man (Deut. 19:11, 13, with Rom. 3:19)
A Runaway from Justice (2 Sam. 13:34, with Gal. 3:10)
In the Place of an Alien (2 Sam. 13:38, with Eph. 2:12)
Grace without Righteousness (Contrast 2 Sam. 14:23, with Rom. 5:21)
Divine Judgment Follows (2 Sam. 18:24, with Prov. 29:1)

212   Solomon, the Wise King

(2 Chronicles 1:1-12)

Solomon, a Type of Christ (2 Chron. 1:8, with Luke 1:32; Ps. 72:1)
His Wealth and Wisdom (2 Chron. 1:12, with Col. 2:3; Eph. 3:8)
His Reign of Peace (1 Kings 5:4, with Isa. 9:6, 7)
His Manifested Glory (1 Kings 9:4, with John 17:24)
His Preeminence (1 Kings 9:23, with Phil. 2:10)

213   The Queen of Sheba

(2 Chronicles 9:1-12)

She heard a Report—Her Awakening
She took a long Journey—Her Earnestness
She met a Wise King—Type of Christ
She opened her Heart—Her Honesty
She asked many Questions—Her Anxiety
She heard his Word—Her Faith
She beheld his Glory—Her Heart Won
She became a Giver—Her Gratitude

> In all these, she is a fine illustration of a sinner disturbed, awakened, hearing of Christ, going to Him, hearing His Word, seeing His Glory, surrendering the heart to Him, and confessing "the half hath not been told."

214 Good King Hezekiah

(2 Chronicles 29:1-19)

His parents were Idolaters—A Bad Example
He lived in a Dark Time—A Day of Iniquity
He was early Converted—His Noble Choice
He took a Decided Stand—His Testimony
He cleansed the Temple—His Work
He restored the Feasts—His Obedience.

215 Josiah, the Young Reformer

(2 Kings 22:1-20; 2 Chronicles 34)

A Young Ruler (v. 1)—A Tender Heart (v. 19)
An Early Conversion (v. 2)—A Good Start
Seeks after God (2 Chron. 34:2)—A Straight Course
A Book Found (v. 11)—A Good Confession
A Sure Promise (v. 20)—A Peaceful End

216 Daniel, the Faithful Witness

(Daniel 1; 4:18; 6:1, 10)

In a Heathen City (Dan. 1:2)—His Captivity
A Purposed Heart (Dan. 1:8)—His Decision
A Noble Decision (Dan. 1:12)—His Testimony
An Envied Ruler (Dan. 6:4)—His Trial
A Faithful Witness (Dan. 6:16)—His Suffering
An Honored Servant (Dan. 6:28)—His Reward

217 Three Noble Princes

(Daniel 3:1, 23)

Godly Companions (Dan. 1:12)—Their Company
Diligent Students (Dan. 1:17)—Their Progress
Favored Servants (Dan. 1:20)—Their Success
True Witnesses (Dan. 3:12)—Their Testimony
Noble Confessors (Dan. 3:18)—Their Decision
Delivered Martyrs (Dan. 3:25)—Their Preservation
Rewarded Sufferers (Dan. 3:30)—Their Promotion

218   **Naaman, the Leper**

(2 Kings 5:1-27)

A Victorious General (v. 1)—His Public Career
A Loathsome Leper (v. 1)—His Private Condition
A Little Captive (v. 2)—A True Witness
A Simple Statement (v. 3)—A Clear Testimony
A Long Journey (v. 6)—His Confessed Need
A Definite Message (v. 10)—His Pride Brought Low
An Angry Retort (v. 11)—His Plans Crossed
A Perfect Cure (v. 14)—His Cleansing
A True Acknowledgment (v. 15)—His Confession

219   **Elijah on Carmel**

(1 Kings 18:20-40)

A Remarkable Assembly (v. 20)—Day of Decision
A Call to Choice (v. 21)—No Neutrality
A Noble Witness (v. 32)—God's Claim Recognized
A Sign from Heaven (v. 38)—God's Answer
A Great Judgment (v. 40)—Divine Retribution

220   **The Widow's Pot of Oil**

(2 Kings 4:1-7)

A Scene of Poverty (v. 1)—The Soul's Need (Luke 7:42)
A Source of Supply (v. 2)—The Gospel of God (Titus 2:11)
A Secret Transaction (v. 4)—Faith's Reception (Rom. 3:24)
A Public Restitution (v. 7)—True Conversion (Luke 19:8)

PETALS FROM THE PSALMS

221   The Happy Man
(Psalm 1)
His Company (v. 1, with Eph. 5:11)
His Occupation (v. 2, with 1 Peter 2:2)
His Appearance (v. 3, with John 15:6)
His Work (v. 3, with 1 Cor. 15:58)

222   Christ in Humiliation and Glory
(Psalm 8)
"Thou hast Made" (v. 5)—Incarnation
"Thou hast Crowned" (v. 5)—Glorification
"Thou hast Put" (v. 6)—Subjection

223   The Words of God
(Psalm 12)
Pure in their Origin (v. 6)
Perfect in their Trial (v. 6)
Powerful in their Effects (v. 7)

224   Two Kinds of Hearts
(Psalm 13)
A Sorrowful Heart (v. 2)—For Sin
A Rejoicing Heart (v. 5)—In Salvation

225   Christ, the Believer's Portion
(Psalm 16)
Christ, the Resting Place of Faith (v. 1)—Trusting
Christ, the Portion of Love (v. 5)—Enjoying
Christ, the Object of Life (v. 8)—Contemplating

226   Blessings of the Gospel

(Psalm 17)

Safe as the Apple of the Eye (v. 8)
Sheltered under the Lord's Shadow (v. 8)
Satisfied with the Lord's Likeness (v. 15)

227   A Wonderful Savior

(Psalm 18)

A Rock of Salvation (v. 2)—To Build on
A Fortress of Security (v. 2)—To Hide in
A High Tower of Sight (v. 2)—To Look from

228   The Power of His Word

(Psalm 19)

In Creation (v. 1)—Originating
In Control (v. 5)—Sustaining
In Conversion (v. 7)—Turning
In Commandment (v. 8)—Controlling

229   The Psalm of the Cross

(Psalm 22)

Forsaken by God (v. 1)
Despised by Men (v. 6)
Compassed by Foes (v. 12)
Opposed by Satan (v. 13)
Pierced by Sinners (v. 16)
Accepted by God (v. 24)

230   The Shepherd and the Sheep

(Psalm 23)

A Personal Shepherd, to Supply (v. 1)
A Trusted Leader, to Control (vv. 2, 3)
A Faithful Companion, to Comfort (v. 4)
A Bountiful Provider, to Gladden (v. 5)
A Loving Householder, to Welcome (v. 6)

231   What the Lord Is

(Psalm 27)

Salvation to the Sinner (v. 1)
Strength to the Weak (v. 1)
Shelter for the Tried (v. 5)
Song to the Delivered (v. 6)

232   The Voice of the Lord

(Psalm 29)

Powerful in Nature (vv. 3, 6)
Praiseful in Redemption (v. 9)
Peaceful in Relationship (v. 11)

233   A Song of Redemption

(Psalm 30)

"Lifted up" from Nature's Fall (v. 1)
"Healed" of Sin's Wounds (v. 2)
"Kept Alive" by Daily Grace (v. 3)
"Girded" with Gladness in Resurrection (v. 11)
"Praising" forever in Glory (v. 12)

234   The Sinner Forgiven

(Psalm 32)

Sin Covered by Atonement (v. 1)
Sin Confessed by the Sinner (v. 5)
Sin Forgiven by God (v. 5)

235   A Gospel Landscape

(Psalm 36)

"Mercy," high as the Heavens (v. 5)
"Faithfulness," extending to the Clouds (v. 5)
"Righteousness," firm as the Mountains (v. 6)
"Judgment," deep as the Seas (v. 6)
"Satisfaction," abundant as Fatness (v. 8)
"Pleasures," flowing as a River (v. 8)

236   A Great Deliverance

(Psalm 40)

Brought out of the Pit (v. 1)—Conversion
Set on the Rock (v. 2)—Position
A Song in the Mouth (v. 3)—Praise
Many shall hear (v. 3)—Confession

237   The King and the Kingdom

(Psalm 45)

The King's Beauty—"Fairer than men" (v. 2)
The King's Voice—"Gracious Words" (v. 4)
The King's Majesty—"Truth and Meekness" (v. 4)
The King's Throne—"Forever and ever" (v. 6)
The King's Scepter—"Righteousness" (v. 6)

238   The King and His Court

(Psalm 45)

The Bride of the King—The Redeemed (v. 1; Rev. 21:9)
The Desire of the King—His Accepted (v. 11; Eph. 1:6)
The Retinue of the King—Honorable (v. 9; 1 Peter 2:9)
The Possession of the King—Thy Lord (v. 11; Phil. 3:9)
The Palace of the King—Heaven (v. 15; Rev. 22)

239   Three Great Gospel Facts

(Psalm 49)

Redemption of Christ (v. 8, with 1 Peter 1:19)
Resurrection of Saints (v. 14, with 1 Cor. 15:52)
Retribution of Sinners (vv. 16, 20, with 2 Peter 2:9)

240 Conviction, Cleansing, Contrition

(Psalm 51)

Conviction of Sin (v. 4)—By the Word
Cleansing from Sin (v. 7)—By the Blood
Contrition for Sin (v. 17)—In the Heart

241 The Godless Man

(Psalm 53)

No God (v. 1)—In his Heart
No Good (v. 3)—By his Hand
No Glory (v. 6)—In his Future

242 The Name of the Lord

(Psalm 54)

Salvation by His Name (v. 1, with Acts 4:12)
Praise to His Name (v. 6)

243 The Higher Rock

(Psalm 61)

A Shelter of Salvation (v. 3)—To which Sinners may
Flee
A Tower of Strength (v. 3)—In which the Helpless are
Secure
A Covert of Security (v. 4)—In which the Believer is
Safe

244 A Temple Psalm

(Psalm 84)

Inside the Court (v. 1)—Salvation
Standing by the Altar (v. 3)—Acceptance
Dwelling in the House (v. 4)—Communion

1. Passing through the one "Door" (John 10:9)
2. Trusting in the one "Sacrifice" (Heb. 10:12)
3. In Subjection to the one "Lord" (Eph. 4:5)

245   The People of God
(Psalm 95)

A Saved People (v. 1)
A Singing People (v. 2)
A Worshiping People (v. 6)
A Shepherded People (v. 7)

    1. Having Christ as their Savior (Luke 1:47)
    2. With Christ as their Song (Rev. 5:9)
    3. The Living Lord, the Object of their Worship (Luke 24:52)
    4. The Great Shepherd, their Leader (Heb. 13:20)

246   God's Benefits
(Psalm 103)

A Bountiful Giver (v. 2)
A Gracious Forgiver (v. 3)
A Mighty Healer (v. 3)
A Great Redeemer (v. 4)
A Rich Satisfier (v. 5)

247   A Picture of God's People
(Psalm 107)

Redeemed by the Lord (v. 2)
Gathered out from the World (v. 3)
Sustained from Heaven (vv. 5,6)
Led on in the Right Way (v. 7)
To an Eternal Dwelling Place (v. 8)

248   The Exalted Christ
(Psalm 110)

A Priest to Succor and Sustain (vv. 1, 4)
A King to Rule and Reign (vv. 2, 3)
A Judge to Pardon or Punish (vv. 5, 6)

    1. "We have such a Great High Priest" (Heb. 8:2)
    2. "The Lord is our King" (Isa. 33:22)
    3. "God shall Judge the Secrets of Men by Jesus Christ" (Rom. 2:10)

249   Creation and Redemption

(Psalm 111)

God's Works display His Power (v. 2)
His Ways commend His Wisdon (v. 4)
His Redemption reveals His Grace (v. 9)

250   Experiences of the Soul

(Psalm 116)

Sorrows of the Sinner (v. 3)
Grace of the Savior (v. 4)
Preservation of the Simple (v. 6)
Rest of the Soul (v. 7)
Rejoicing in God's Salvation (v. 13)
Death of the Saint (v. 15)

251   The Keeper and the Kept

(Psalm 121)

A Mighty Helper (v. 2)
A Strong Supporter (v. 3)
A Watchful Keeper (v. 4)
A Sheltering Shade (v. 5)
A Soul Preserver (v. 7)
An External Protector (v. 8)

252   A Song of Deliverance

(Psalm 126)

A Joyful Deliverance (v. 1)
A Gladsome Confession (v. 2)
An Earnest Supplication (v. 3)
A Happy Consummation (v. 4)

253   The Backslider's Wail

(Psalm 137)

Captives in Babylon (v. 1)—No Rest
Harps on the Willows (v. 2)—No Song
Scorned by Captors (v. 3)—No Testimony
Condition Felt (v. 4)—Conviction
Home Remembered (v. 5)—Restoration

254   From Nature to God

(Psalm 144)

Brevity of Human Life—"A Shadow" (v. 4)
Might of Delivering Power—"Thine Hand" (v. 7)
Praise for God's Salvation—"A New Song" (v. 9)
Joy of Christian Life—"Happy People" (v. 15)

255   The Mighty God

(Psalm 145)

His Greatness (v. 8)—To be Owned
His Goodness (v. 9)—To be Proved
His Glory (v. 11)—To be Exalted

256   The Last "Hallelujah"

(Psalm 150)

Praise of Worshipers, in the Sanctuary (v. 1)
Praise of Angels, in the Heavens (v. 1)
Praise of Beholders, for His Works (v. 2)
Praise of Admirers, in His Person (v. 2)
Praise of all Creation, Universal (v. 6)

PEBBLES FROM THE PROPHETS

257   An Utter Ruin

(The sinner described in Isaiah 1:6)

The Head Sick—Sin in Thought (Eph. 2:3)
The Heart Faint—Sin in Desire (Jer. 17:9)
The Body Bruised—Sin in Life (Luke 4:18)
The Sores Corrupt—Sin in Death (James 1:15)

258   A Gracious Invitation

(Isaiah 1:18)

A Call from God, "Come"—Divine Invitation (Luke 14:17)
A Set Time, "Now"—Time of Grace (2 Cor. 6:2)
A Subject to Discuss, "Let us Reason"—Divine Kindness (Titus 3:5)

259   A Prophet's Vision

(Isaiah 6:1-4)

A Lofty Throne (v. 1)—Divine Majesty
A Temple Filled (v. 1)—Divine Holiness
A Door Moved (v. 4)—Divine Power

     1. Sinners must meet it here or hereafter (Rom. 20:12)
     2. Without holiness no man shall see the Lord (Heb. 12:14)
     3. He both opens and shuts the Door of Grace (Luke 13:25)

260   Three Personal Experiences

(Isaiah 6:5-9)

Conviction of Sin (v. 5)—"I am Undone"
Cleansing through Sacrifice (v. 6)—"Thy Sin is Purged"
Commissioned To Serve (v. 9)—"Go and Tell"
> 1. True Conviction is by the Spirit and Word of God (John 16:8)
> 2. Divine Cleansing is through the Blood of Christ (1 John 1:7)
> 3. Only the Saved are sent to Serve (1 Thess. 1:9)

261   Christ and His Glories

(Isaiah 9:6-7)

A Child Born—His Incarnation (Matt. 1:23)
A Son Given—His Divine Glory (John 3:16)
A Counsellor to Guide—His Perfect Wisdom (Prov. 8:30)
A Prince to Pacify—His Atoning Work (Col. 1:20)
A King to Govern—His Almighty Power (Ps. 72)

262   A Song of Salvation

(Isaiah 12)

Anger Turned Away (v. 1)—At the Cross (1 Thess. 1:10)
Salvation Brought Nigh (v. 2)—By the Gospel (Eph. 1:13)
Refreshment Opened Up (v. 2)—In the Word (Col. 3:16)
Praise Goes Up (v. 4)—To the Lord (Heb. 13:15)
Testimony Goes Forth (v. 4)—To the World (Mark 15:16)

263   The Watchman's Message

(Isaiah 21:11-12)

A Scoffer's Question (v. 11)—"What of the Night?"
A Dawn of Glory (v. 12)—"The Morning Cometh"
A Night of Judgment (v. 12)—"Also the Night"
A Call to Repentance (v. 12)—"Return, Come"

264 A Model Dwelling for the Believer

(Isaiah 26:1-4)

A Strong City (v. 1)—His Home (John 14:2)
Salvation Walls (v. 1)—His Security (John 10:28)
Open Gates (v. 2)—His Liberty (John 10:9)
Peaceful Dwelling (v. 3)—His Experience (Phil. 4:7)
A God to Trust (v. 4)—His Resource (Ps. 46:1)

265　True and False Security

(Isaiah 28:14-18)

A Sure Foundation (v. 16)— Christ, the Rock
A Saving Confidence (v. 16)—"He that Believeth"

These describe Christ and the Trusting Soul.

A False Security (v. 17)—"A Refuge of Lies"
A Sudden Sweep (v. 17)—Judgment to Come

These describe the Sinner and his Judgment

266　An Indictment and a Pardon

(Isaiah 43:23-25)

God's Claims not met (v. 23)—The Sinner's Omissions
Sins and Iniquities Weary Him (v. 24)—The Sinner's
　Commissions
God's Abounding Grace (v. 26)—"I am He that blotteth
　out"
The Only Cause (v. 25)—"For Mine own sake"

267　The Substitute and Sin-bearer

(Isaiah 53)

His Attitude Godward (v. 2)—Grows up before Him
His Relation Man (v. 3)—Despised and Rejected
His Sufferings as Surety (v. 5)—Wounded for
　Transgressors
His Burden as Sin-bearer (v. 6)—Iniquity laid on Him
His Death as Substitute (v. 8)—Stricken for His People

268   A Call From Heaven

(Isaiah 55:1-2)

To the Thirsty (v. 1)—Come to the Waters
To the Hungry (v. 2)—Eat that which is good
To the Unsatisfied (v. 3)—Delight in Fatness

> In Christ the threefold need is abundantly met:
> He has the Water of Life to give (John 4:14)
> He is the Bread of Life to feed upon (John 6:35)
> He is the Satisfier of the Heart (Phil. 3:8)

269   Abundant Pardon

(Isaiah 55:7)

A Call to Repentance—"Forsake his way" (Prov. 14:12)
An Invitation to Grace—"Return to the Lord" (1 Thess. 1:10)
A Promise of Mercy—"He will have Mercy" (Eph. 2:4)
A Gracious Pardon—"Abundantly Pardon" (Col. 3:13)

270   The Great Deliverer

(Isaiah 61:11, with Like 4:18,21)

A Promised Deliverer—"Christ, the Anointed" (Rom. 11:26)
A Gracious Message—"Good Tidings" (Luke 2:10)
A Period of Grace—"Acceptable Year" (2 Cor. 6:2)
A Day of Retribution—"Day of Vengeance" (2 Thess. 1:8)

271   The Bridegroom's Gifts

(Isaiah 61:10-11)

"Garments of Salvation"—For Sinners (1 Tim. 1:15)
"Robes of Righteousness"—for Unrighteous (2 Cor. 5:21)
"Ornaments of Grace"—For the Life (1 Peter 3:4, 7)
"Jewels of Glory"—For Heaven (John 17:22)

272   Treading the Winepress

(Isaiah 63:3)

Glorious in Apparel—Christ in Glory (Rev. 19:11)
Great in Strength—Christ in Power (Rev. 12:10)
Speaking in Righteousness—Christ as Judge (Rev. 19:11)
Treading the Winepress—Christ as Avenger (Rev. 19:13)
Mighty to Save—Christ as Deliverer (Zech. 12:8)

273   Divine Mercy and Loving Kindness

(Isaiah 63:7-11)

His Loving Kindness—Manifested in Gift of Christ
  (Rom. 5:8)
The Afflicted Savior—Christ our Sacrifice (Isaiah 53:4)
A Great Redemption—By His Blood (1 Peter 1:19)
Carried all the Days—By His Power (Luke 15:5)

274   Jerusalem, the Golden

(Isaiah 65:19-25)

A New Creation (v. 18; Rev. 21:2, 5)
A Joyful City (v. 18; Rev. 21:3)
A Joyed over People (v. 19; Zeph. 3:17)
No more Weeping (v. 19; Rev. 21:4)
Length of Days (v. 20; Rev. 22:5)
Peace and Prosperity (v. 25; Rev. 21:24)

275 Jeremiah's Call and Commission

(Jeremiah 1:1-19)

"I Knew Thee"—Predestination (Rom. 8:29)
"I Formed Thee"—Regeneration (John 3:7)
"I Sanctified Thee"—Separation (1 Cor. 6:10)
"I Ordained Thee"—Commission (Matt. 28:18)

In these four points, he resembles the saved sinner, and in their spiritual order, his history.

276 A Living Fountain and Broken Cisterns

The Living Fountain—God the Source of Blessing
(Rev. 21:6)
Man Forsaking Him—The Sinner's Path (Isa. 53:6)
Broken Cisterns—The World's Pleasures (John 4:13)
Hewn by Labor—The Sinner's Toil (Isa. 55:2)
A Great Invitation (Isa. 55:1)—The Last Call
(Rev. 22:17)

277 A Call to Backsliders

(Jeremiah 3:6-25)

A Backslider Described (v. 6)—God Forsaken, Sin
Indulged
Self Justification (v. 11)—Hardened and Unrepentant
God's Call to Repentance (v. 18)—"Acknowledge thine
Iniquity"
Relationship Owned (v. 14)—"I am married to you"
Divine Restoration (v. 14)—"I will bring you"
A Gracious Result (v. 22)—"I will heal"
A Full Confession (v. 25)—"We have sinned"

278 A False Peace

(Jeremiah 8:6-11)

God Hearkening (v. 6)—He knows all (Ezek. 35:12)
Sinners Rusking on (v. 6)—The End, Destruction (Rom.
3:16)
No Conviction of Sin (v. 6)—Utter Indifference (Ps.
13:4)
Slightly Healed (v. 11)—Unreal Profession (Titus 1:11)
A Hollow Peace (v. 11)—False Security (Rom. 3:17)
Rudely Broken (v. 12)—Coming Judgment (1 Thess. 5:2)

279   The Wail of the Christ Rejecter

(Jeremiah 8:16-22)

Sounds of Coming Judgment (v. 16)—The Sinner's Fear

Divine Vengeance Announced (v. 17)—The Sure
Fulfilment

A Harvest of Grace Neglected (v. 20)—Salvation
Despised

A Summer of Opportunity Ended (v. 20)—Grace
Neglected

Balm in Gilead (v. 22)—Gospel Power Refused

A Great Physician (v. 22)—Christ Rejected

280   The Swelling of Jordan

(Jeremiah 12:1-7)

The River of Jordan—Figure of Death (Josh. 3:1)

Swollen in Flood—Death in Power (Ps. 55:4)

Passing Through it—The Sinner's Death (Luke 16:22)

Jordan Cut Off (Josh. 2:15)—Christ Abolished it (2 Tim.
1:10)

Pass Over Dry Shod (Josh. 2:17)—Believer's Passage
(Phil. 1:23)

281   The Potter and His Vessels

(Jeremiah 18:1-12)

The Potter at Work—God in Creation (Gen. 1:26)

The Vessel Made—Man Made Upright (Eccl. 7:29)

The Vessel Marred—Man's Ruin (Rom. 5:12)

The Vessel Re-made—Man Regenerated (John 3:7)

A Vessel of Mercy (Rom. 9:22)—A New Creation (2 Cor.
5:17)

For a Great Future—Prepared for Glory (1 Peter 5:10)

282 Ways of Life and Death

(Jeremiah 21:1-14)

"Way of Life" (with Matt. 7:13)—Definition
"Go Forth" (with John 10:9)—Decision
"He shall Live" (with John 3:36)—Possession
"Way of Death" (with Matt. 7:14)—The End
"He that Abideth" (with Prov. 21:16)—The Path
"Shall Die" (with Prov. 29:1)—The Doom

283 A Sermon in a Palace

(Jeremiah 22:1-19)

A Faithful Preacher (v. 2)
A Solemn Warning (vv. 7, 9)
A Definite Message (vv. 3, 5)
A Hopeless Death (vv. 10, 12)
A Loveless Grave (vv. 18, 19)

284 The Lord, Our Righteousness

(Jeremiah 23:1-8)

The Promised Deliverer (v. 7, with Luke 2:11)
The Saying Name (v. 8, with Cor. 1:30)
The Great Restorer (v. 8, with Luke 4:18)

285 Everlasting Love

(Jeremiah 30:1-14)

"Loved" (with Rom. 5:8)—The Source
"Drawn" (with John 6:44)—The Power
"Brought" (with Luke 15:16)—The Means
"Kept" (with 1 Peter 1:5)—The Security

286   A Story of Grace

(Ezekiel 16:1-14)

State by Nature (v. 3)—The Sinner (Eph. 2:3)
Place of Destitution (v. 5)—His State (Eph. 2:12)
An Object of Love (v. 6)—His Favor (Eph. 2:4)
A Great Salvation (vv. 8, 9)—His Blessing (Titus 2:11)
A Complete Renovation (vv. 10, 14)—His Standing
  (Eph. 1:3, 6)

287   The Watchman and His Message

(Ezekiel 33:1-11)

A Watchman's Work (v. 2, with Acts 20:26, 27)
A Coming Judgment (v. 3, with Heb. 9:27)
A Clear Call (v. 4, with Acts 17:3)
A Double Result (v. 8, 9, with John 3:36)
A Divine Assurance (v. 11, with 2 Peter 3:9, 10)

288   Story of a Runaway

(Jonah 1 and 2)

Fleeing from the Lord (Jonah 1:3, with Ps. 139:7)
Favorable Circumstances (Jonah 1:3, with Luke 17:28, 29)
Aroused and Convicted (Jonah 1:6, 10, with Acts 16:29, 30)
Prayer and Vows (Jonah 2:1, 6, with Titus 3:5)
Salvation and Liberty (Jonah 2:9, 10, with Col. 1:13)

289   A Solemn Appeal

(Amos 4:12)

All *must* meet God in Grace or Judgment (Rom. 3:25;
  Acts 17:11)
Some *are* Prepared, others *not* (Matt. 25:10, 11)
How to be Prepared (2 Cor. 5:20; Col. 1:21)

290   From Filthy Garments to a Fair Crown

(Zechariah 3:1-8)

Standing Before the Lord—The Right Place (Micah 6:6)
Satan Resisting—The Adversary's Work (1 Thess. 2:18)
Clad in Filthy Garments—Human Righteousness (Isa. 64:6)
Stripped of All—A True Position (Job 40:4)
Cleansed from Sin—A Great Relief (1 Cor. 4:11)
Clothed with Righteousness—A New Standing (2 Cor. 5:21)
Crowned as a Priest—A True Worshiper (1 Peter 2:5, 9)

GEMS FROM THE GOSPELS

291 **The Promised Savior**

(Matthew 1; 2:1)

Who? **B**ORN of Abraham's Seed (Gal. 3:16)
Where? in David's City (Micah 5:2)
How? of a Virgin (Isa. 7:14)

292 **Visit of the Wise Men**

(Matthew 2:1-11)

Wise Men   Seekers   Looking for
elcome Him   Travellers   Led to   **J**ESUS
orship Him   Givers   Give unto

293 **A Desert Preacher**

(Matthew 3:1-12)

A Plain Preacher   **C**onvicted of sins
ointed Message   onfess them to God
repared People   onverted in Life

294 **The Baptism of Jesus**

(Matthew 3:13-17)

John, the Baptizer   Son obeys—Example
esus, the Baptized   **T**HE Father Approves—Word
ordan, the Place   Spirit descends—Seal

295   The Great Temptation

(Matthew 4:1-12)

Threefold Temptation, as	Way of Victory	The
Son of Man	**W**ord of God Weapon	**D**efeated
overeign	ill of God Rule	evil
on of God	ay of God Path	eparts

296   The First Disciples

(Matthew 4:18-22)

Companions in Youth   **S**inners by Nature
onverted at same time   aints by Grace
alled to serve Christ   ervants by Calling

297   Two Roads and Two Destinies

(Matthew 7:13-24)

Birth in Sin—Start   **S**trait Gate—Conversion
road Road—Course   aved—Condition
lackness—End   ealed for Glory—Goal

298   Two Builders and Their Houses

(Matthew 7:24-29)

Sand Foundation   **R**ock of Salvation
hallow Profession   esting by Faith
wept Away   aised to Glory

299   Pharisees and Publicans

(Matthew 9:10-13)

Pharisees, Religious **S**inners   **R**ejected
ublicans, Wicked   elf-righteous   eceived

300 Levi, the Taxgatherer

(Matthew 9:9)

Called by
Christ while he sat at
Custom

Responded to His Call
Received His Word
Resigned His Post

301 A Ruler's Little Girl

(Matthew 9:18-26)

Faith's Assurance—"She shall live"
Father's Request—"Come"

JESUS Came
JESUS Spoke

302 The Cities by the Lake

(Matthew 11:20-30)

Privileged Cities
Person of Christ seen
Power of Christ known

Refused His Words
Rejected Warnings
Repented Not

303 A Woman of Canaan

(Matthew 15:2-31)

An Alien
An Earnest

Sinner
Seeker

Came to Right Person
Came in the Wrong Way

304 Peter's Confession

(Matthew 16:13-28)

A Question asked
An Answer given
A Revelation made

Christ revealed
Confessed by Peter
Church built on the Rock

305 A Savior Born

(Luke 2:1-7)

Sung in heaven
Sent to Bethlehem
Suffered at Calvary

NO ROOM
in the Inn
in World
in Heart

306   The Angel and the Shepherds
(Luke 2:8-20)

Angel
nnounced
dvent

Good Tidings
reat Joy
lory to God

Shepherds Hear
ee the Savior
pread the News

307   Aged Lovers of Christ
(Luke 2:25-39)

Simeon Waiting
Anna Serving

Saw the Savior
pake of Him

Took Him
hanked God

308   The Boy of Nazareth
(Luke 2:41-50)

Jesus
ourneyed to
erusalem

Parents
artook of
assover

At the Feast
mong Doctors
t Home

309   Jesus at Nazareth
(Luke 4:15-31)

Preaches Gospel
roclaims Liberty

Mission despised
essage rejected

310   Peter's Conversion and Call
(Luke 5:1-11)

Convicted of Sin
onfesses his State

His **D**ecision
His **D**evotion

311   The Centurion's Servant
(Luke 7:1-10)

Soldier's
ick
ervant

Hears of
Sends to
Trusts in

JESUS

Hears
onors
eals

312   The Young Man of Nain
(Luke 7:11-18)

Dead Youth   **W**eeping   **W**ord of Love
Distressed People   **W**idow   **W**ord of Power

313   The Elder Brother
(Luke 15:25-32)

Self-righteousness   **J**udges his Father
Serving Legally   **J**ustifies Himself
Self Satisfied   **J**ealous of his Brother

314   The Rich Man and Lazarus
Luke 16:10-31)

Two
Men—Rich and Poor
Lives—Christless and Christian
Deaths—In Sin and in Faith
Destinies—Heaven or Hell

315   The Ten Lepers
(Luke 17:11-19)

A Leper   **S**inner   **C**hrist
   far off   **S**eparated   **C**leanses
Among   **S**hut out   **C**laims

316   The Pharisee and Publican
(Luke 18:9-14)

Pharisee, Self-righteous   **P**ublican Confesses
Prayer, Self-sufficient   **P**osition, Stands Off
Posture, Self-reliant   **P**leads for Mercy

317   Jesus and the Children
(Luke 18: 15-17)

Who speaks? Jesus   **W**ho are called? Children
What says He? Come   **W**hen? In Early Years
Where? "Unto Me"   **W**hy? Of such is the Kingdom

318   A Rich Young Man

(Luke 18:18-30)

UN_satisfying_ Riches   **R**_iches_ of Mercy
     searchable Riches   _iches_ of Grace

319   The Blind Beggar

(Luke 19: 35-43)

Without Christ   From Christ   With Christ

D_arkness_   **S**_ight_   **D**_iscipleship_
D_estitution_   **S**_alvation_   **D**_evotedness_

320   Zaccheus, the Publican

(Luke 19:1-10)

Seeks   **C**ould not   Receives
Sees   **J**ESUS   limbs up   Confesses   **H**IM
Saved   comes   Owns
_by_   down

321   The Nobleman and His Servants

(Luke 19:11-27)

Noblemen   Citizens   Servants

C_hrist_   **D**_espised_   **R**_eceived_
 rucified   _isowned_   _emained_
 rowned   _isobeyed_   _eturned_
 oming   _estroyed_   _ewarded_

322   Vineyard and Husbandmen

(Luke 20:21-26)

S_ervants_ sent to Seek—Law   **D**_isobeyed_
 _on_ sent to Save—Grace   _espised_
 pirit sent to strive—Gospel   _espited_

323   Judas, the Traitor

(Luke 22:1-6, 47-48; Acts 1)

Professed to be a disciple
reached to others
erished at last

Coveted
ovenanted with Priests
ommitted suicide

324   Garden of Gethsemane

(Luke 22:39-53)

Place

Scene of
avior's
orrow

Persons

Suffering Savior
leeping Disciples
trengthening Angel

325   Jesus and Peter

(Luke 22:31-34, 54-62)

Jesus

Sweating in Agony
uffering in Submission
ilent in Confidence

Peter

Sleeping in Ease
miting in Vengeance
wearing in Anger

326   Pilate's Decision

(Luke 23:1-4, 13-16)

Priests Demand Death
ilate Perplexed
eople's Voice prevails

Conscience awake
hoice must be made
hrist or Barabbas

327   Green Tree and Dry

(Luke 23:26-31)

Bearing Fruit
eautiful to God

Burned (Heb. 6:8)
arren (Luke 13:7)

328   **Two Robbers**

(Luke 23:33, 39-41)

Christ Accepter	*Christ Rejecter*
Owns Guilt	Demands Deliverance
Justifies Christ	Scoffs at Christ
Confesses Him	Rails Against
Is Owned by Him	No Repentance
Goes to be with Him	Dies in Sin

329   **Groups Around the Cross**

(Luke 23:33-36)

Foes	*Christ*
Rulers, deriding	**S**acrifice for sin
Soldiers, mocking	**S**ubstitute for sinners
People, beholding	**S**urety for Saints

330   **The Resurrection of Christ**

(Luke 24:1-12)

RAISED by the Father / by Himself / by the Spirit   **P**roof of sin put away / rospect of Victory / ledge of Resurrection

331 Results of Death and Resurrection

(Luke 24:36-53)

Peace Proclaimed / ardon Imparted / ower Bestowed   **P**riestly Blessing Given / arted from them / raise Ascending

MESSAGES FROM THE MIRACLES

332   Water Turned to Wine

Wine, the Emblem of Joy (Ps. 104:15; 4:7)
The Supply Fails (Eccl. 2:10)
Jesus Provides It (John 15:11)
In Full Measure (1 Peter 1:18)
Water, the Emblem of the Word (Rev. 22:17)
Believed, it Brings Joy (Rom. 15:13)

333   A Nobleman's Son Healed

(John 4:46-56)

"At the point of Death"—Like the Sinner (Heb. 9:27)
"Come Down"—The Appeal of Need (Rom. 10:12)
"Thy Son Liveth"—The Healing Word (Ps. 107:20)
"The Man Believed the Word"—Faith (John 5:24)
"The same Hour"—Definite Time of Conversion (Luke 19:9)
"Amend"—Man's Way. "Fever left him"—God's Way
   (Eccl. 3:14)

334 A Palsied Man Forgiven and Cured

(Luke 5:17-26)

The Needy Man, Guilty, Diseased—The Sinner
The Bringers had Faith, sought Means—The Workers
The Mighty Healer speaks Forgiveness—The Savior
The Religious Onlookers, Cavil—The Opposers
The Healed Man, Forgiven, Raised up—The Saved

335 **The Storm Calmed**

(Mark 4:35-41)

The Voyage of Life (v. 35)—"Let us Pass Over"
Jesus with His own (v. 36)—"He was in the Ship"
The Storms of Life (v. 37)—"A Great Storm"
The Fears of Unbelief (v. 38)—"Carest Thou Not?"
The Word of Power (v. 39)—"Peace, be still"
A Pleasant Change (v. 39)—"A Great Calm"

> The sinner's awakening, fear, danger, cry of need; the power of
> Christ, the Gospel of peace, the calm of confidence, enjoyment of
> peace and passage to glory are all foreshadowed here.

336 **The Man of Gadara**

(Mark 5:1-21)

In the Devil's Grasp (v. 2)—The Sinner's Position
Living among the Dead (v. 2)—The Sinner's Place
Could not be Restrained (v. 3)—The Sinner's State
Could not be Reformed (v. 4)—Man's Inability
Jesus, the Mighty Healer (v. 6)—Jesus Near
Demons dread His Power (v. 7)—Satan's Opposition
A Great Deliverance (v. 8)—Personal Salvation
A Testimony to Christ (v. 16)—Manifest Conversion
A Witness for Christ (vv. 19, 20)—True Discipleship

337 **A Chronic Case Cured**

(Mark 5:25-34)

A Disease of long Continuance (v. 25)
A Patient of many Physicians (v. 26)
A Case of continuous Decline (v. 26)
A Crisis in ruined Resources (v. 26)
Hears of a new Healer (v. 27)
Came into touch with Christ (v. 27)
Healed by His Power, and knew it (v. 29)
Confessed it, and was owned by Him (v. 34)

338   Five Thousand Fed

(Mark 6:30-34)

A Hungry Crowd (v. 34)—Mankind
A Desert Place (v. 36)—The World
A Declining Day (v. 35)—Brevity of Life
The Divine Compassion (v. 37)—Grace of God
A Resting People (v. 40)—Not by Works
A Miracle of Power (v. 41)—Power of Christ
An Abundant Supply (v. 42)—Abundant Salvation

339   Jesus Walks Across the Sea

(Mark 4:45-50)

A Lone Night (v. 47)—The Present Time
A Stormy Sea (v. 48). The Storm of Life
A Topling Crew (v. 48)—The Church on Earth
A Praying Lord (v. 47)—In Heaven
A Timely Deliverer (v. 49)—The Coming One
A Word of Cheer (v. 50)—His own Voice
A Presence of Power (v. 51)—Himself in the Midst

340   A Blind Man Receives Sight

(Mark 8:22-30)

A Blind Man (v. 22)—Sinner in Nature
A Call of Need (v. 22)—Praying Saints
A Touch of Tenderness (v. 23)—Christ's Compassion
A Work Begun (v. 23)—The Spirit's Work
A Dawning Light (v. 24)—The Enlightening Word
A Clear Vision (v. 26)—A True Salvation

341   A Demon Possessed Lad

(Mark 9:14-29)

An Anxious Father (v. 17)—Man of Faith
A Needy Son (v. 18)—Under Satan's Power
Helpless Disciples (v. 14-28)—Disputing among
   Themselves (v. 33)
A Mighty Deliverer (v. 19)—Jesus Christ

342   A Helpless Man Healed

(John 5:1-6)

A Waiting Company (v. 3)—In Conscious Need
A Place of Disappointment (v. 4)—Ordinances Cannot
   Save
A Divine Visitor (v. 6)—The Living Lord
A Personal Question (v. 6)—"Wilt thou be made
   Whole?"
A Voice of Power (v. 8)—"Rise," "Walk"
A Sudden Response (v. 9)—Saved to show it

343   The Ten Lepers

(Luke 17:11-17)

An Urgent Appeal—"Have mercy on us"
A Ready Response—Jesus saw and spake
A Great Result—"They were cleansed"
A Grateful Return—One returned to give thanks

344   Bartimaeus, the Beggar

(Luke 18:35)

In Nature, Blind and Destitute (Acts 26:18)
Near to Jericho, City of the Curse (Gal. 3:10)
Jesus Passing by, the Gospel now (Acts 15:14)
Is Called and Responds (Matt. 11:28)
Receives Sight and Salvation (2 Cor. 4:6)
Follows in the Way (Ps. 23:1)

345   Lazarus of Bethany

(John 11:1-46)

Dead and Decomposing—Our Condition (Eph. 2:1; 4:22)

Bound and Buried—Our Helplessness (John 8:34; Rom. 5:6)

The Stone Rolled Away—What Man can do (John 1:41, 42)

The Life-Giver Speaks—Christ's Word of Power (John 5:25)

Life Received and Manifested—Conversion (1 Thess. 1:9; Acts 11:21)

346   Three Resurrection Miracles

(Luke 8, Luke 7, John 11)

Jairus' Daughter—A Girl, Newly Dead

The Widow's Son—A Youth, on the way to Burial

Lazarus—A Man, in the Grave Four Days

> The Sinner dead in sin by nature, becomes immured to it in practice, and held fast by it at the end. Each a stage further advanced in helpless, hopeless ruin. Christ's voice reaches all. His power raises all.

PEARLS FROM THE PARABLES

347   The Patch on the Old Garment

(Mark 2:16-22)

The Old Garment—The Sinner in Nature, the Old Man
A New Patch—Religion or Reformation from Without
Result, a Rent—Only Manifests the Unrenewed Nature
A Great Necessity—A New Birth, Regeneration (John
   3:7)

348   The Seed That Grew

(Mark 4:26-34)

The Seed Sown—The Word enters the heart (1 Peter 1:23)
The Slow Progress—The Dying and Quickening (1 Cor.
   15:36)
The Sure Result—The Manifested Life (Acts 11:22, 23)
The Ripe Harvest—The Full Fruitage (John 4:35)

349   The Two Debtors

(Luke 7:36-50)

Pharisee and Sinner—Religious and Profane (Luke 18:10)
Five Hundred Pence—Great Debt, Openly Ungodly
   (1 Tim. 1:15)
Fifty Pence—Relatively Small, Self-righteous (Luke
   16:15)
"Nothing to Pay"—Alike Bankrupt, no Difference
   (Rom. 3:23)
"Frankly Forgave Both"—Grace to the Guilty, no
   Difference (Rom. 10:12)

350   The Good Samaritan

(Luke 10:30-38)

The Man Going Down—The Sinner's Path
Jerusalem to Jericho—From the Blessing to the Curse
Fell among Thieves—Sin, Satan, the World
Robbed, Stripped, Wounded—Man Fallen, Ruined,
  Helpless
Priest and Levite—Law and Ordinances cannot Save
Samaritan came where he was—Christ on Calvary
Rescued, Bound, Raised—The Believing Sinner's
  Position
Brought, Cared for, Waiting—The Believer's Place and
  Portion

351   The Wealthy Farmer

(Luke 12:16-21)

A Prosperous Man—Rich Crops, Great Success
A Planning Man—Builds Barns, Seeks Ease
A Short-sighted Man—Only for Time! Nothing for
  Eternity
A "Fool" in God's Sight—The Verdict of Heaven
A Sudden Call—That Night in the Eternal World

352   A Barren Fig Tree

(Luke 13:6-9)

In Place of Privilege—Planted in Vineyard
An Object of Pity—Received Owner's Care
A Worthless Possession—Bore no Fruit
An Earnest Appeal—"Let it Alone"
A Year of Grace—Special Visitation
The Final Doom—Cut Down, Cast Out

353   The Gospel Supper

(Luke 14:16-24)

A Gracious Host—God in Grace, Providing (John 3:16)
A Great Invitation—"Come," the Gospel Feast Ready
  (1 Tim. 1:15)
Some Paltry Excuses—Trivial, showing they had no
  desire
A Wider Call—To the Outcasts and Needy
A Motley Company—All Sorts and Conditions

354   The Sheep That Wandered

(Luke 15:1-7)

It Left the Fold—The Sinner Rebellious (Ps. 119:176)
It Wandered Away—The Sinner Self-willed (Isa. 53:6)
It was Lost—His Relation to God (Jer. 50:6)
It was Sought—The Mission of Christ (Luke 19:11)
It was Found—The Sinner Saved (Deut. 32:10)

355   The Silver Piece That Was Lost

(Luke 15:8-10)

Fallen from its Place—Sinners Helpless and Hidden
Lost in the House—In the Place of Profession
The Woman's Diligence—Human Means Used
Light and Sweeping—The Spirit and the Word
Found and Replaced—Sinner Restored to God and Man
Time of Rejoicing—Joy over Conversions

356 The Prodigal's Departure and Degradation

(Luke 15:11-17)

His Departure (v. 13)—"Into a far Country"
His Dissipation (v. 13)—"Riotous Living"
His Degradation (v. 15)—"Sent to Feed Swine"
His Declaration (v. 17)—"I Perish"
His Dejection (v. 16)—"How many Hired Servants"

357 The Prodigal's Return and Reception

(Luke 15:18-32)

His Resolution (v. 18)—"I will Arise"
His Return (v. 19)—"He Arose and Came"
His Reception (v. 20)—"Fell on his neck and kissed him"
His Rejoicing (v. 24)—"They began to be Merry"

358 The Shepherd and His Flock

(John 10:1-28)

The Door of Entrance (v. 9)—Christ Himself
The Number of the Sheep (v. 9)—Individual Salvation
The Shepherd's Register (v. 14)—"I know my Sheep"
The True Sheep Mark (v. 27)—"They hear His Voice"
The Perfect Security (v. 28)—"Never Perish"
Their Sure Possession (v. 28)—"Eternal Life"

TRUTHS IN ACROSTICS

A Bible picture, a blackboard sketch, or an object may be used to illustrate the lesson, with good effect.

359 The Beautiful Garden
(Genesis 2:8-17)

Planted by God
    repared for Man
    leasant and Pure

Tree of Life
    he Flowing River
    rue Happiness

Use as a type of heaven, showing comparisons and contrasts.

360 Abel and His Offering
(Genesis 3:4; Hebrews 11:4)

A *cknowledged* his Sin before God

B *rought* a Sacrifice to God to Atone

E *xercised* Faith in God's Promise

L *ife* and Righteousness reckoned his

361 Noah's Ark Like Jesus
(Genesis 6, 7)

A *place* of Safety
  ll in it Secure

R *efuge* from the Storm
  aised to the Mount

K *ept* from Perishing by God's Power
  ept from Famishing by God's Food

362   The Rainbow and its Lessons
(Genesis 9:8-17)

B ow without an Arrow—No Judgment
right amid the Darkness—Token of Grace

O *nly* Half of it seen by us
ther Half seen in Heaven (Rev. 4:3)

W *itness* of God's Faithfulness
ill never bring another Deluge

363   The Story of Isaac
(Genesis 22; Hebrews 11:17)

I *saac,* the Beloved Son (John 3:16)

S *ubject* to his Father's Will (Hebrews 10:9)

A *Victim* laid on the Altar (Isa. 53:5)

A *Substitute* Died in his Stead (Rom. 5:8)

C *alled* to Heavenly Glory (Hebrews 5:4, 5)

364   The Blood on the Door Posts
(Exodus 12:12-13)

B *eginning* of a New Life (John 3:3)

L *amb* Chosen and Slain (1 Peter 1:18-28)

O *n* Lintel and Side Posts Sprinkled (Hebrews 11:28)

O *nly* Way of Redemption and Safety (Romans 3:25)

D *elivered* from Death and Judgment (Hebrews 9:27)

365   **The Smitten Rock**
(Exodus 17:1; Corinthians 10:4)

Rivers in the Desert (Psalm 105:41; John 7:39)

Opened by God, for Man (Psalm 105:20)

Call to all to Drink (Isaiah 55:1; Rev. 22:17)

Knew its Life-giving Power (Isaiah 48:21)

366   **The Serpent on the Pole**
(Numbers 21:6-10; John 3:14-15)

Lifted up where all might see it (v. 8)

Irremediable Condition of People (v. 6)

Faith in the Word of God (v. 8)

Everyone that Looked, got Life (v. 9)

367   **The Gospel Alphabet**

A ll have Sinned (Romans 3:23)
ll may be Saved (1 Tim. 2:4-6)

B ehold the Lamb of God (John 1:29)
elieve on the Lord Jesus Christ (Acts 16:31)

C ome, for all things are now ready (Luke 15:17)
onfess with thy mouth the Lord Jesus (Romans 10)

368   **Gospel "I Am's"**

I AM the Door (John 10:9)—to Enter by
the Way (John 14:6)—to Walk in
the Shepherd (John 10:11)—to Follow
the Light (John 8:12)—to Guide

369   Three Relations

CHRIST

Received as Savior (John 1:12)
Confessed as Lord (Romans 10:9)
Followed as Shepherd (John 10:27)

370   Three Great R's

(Job 34:24)

Ruin by Sin
ansom by Blood
escue by Power

371   The Gift of God

(Romans 6:23)

Given without asking (John 3:16)

In spite of our sin (1 John 4:10)

Free to all alike (Rev. 22:17)

Take it and thank the Giver (2 Cor. 9:15)

372   Four "I Will's"

I WILL
give you rest (Matt. 11:28)
in no wise cast out (John 6:37)
receive you (John 14:3)
never leave you (Hebrews 13:5)

373   All

All we, like sheep, have gone astray (Isaiah 53:6)

Laid upon Him the iniquity of us ALL (Isaiah 53:6)

Lord of ALL (Acts 10:36)

Our Sin, His Sacrifice, His Lordship

374 **Hath**

He that Heareth My Word

And Believeth on Him

That sent Me

Hath Everlasting Life—John 5:24

The three go together—Heareth, Believeth, Hath

375 **Jesus**

Son of God (Matt. 3:17)—Well Beloved
acrifice for God (Eph. 5:2)—Well Pleasing
avior of Sinners (Hebrews 7:25)—All Powerful

376 **Christ for Me**

The Work of Christ gives Peace (Col. 1:20)
The Word of Christ gives Assurance (John 5:24)
The Person of Christ gives Satisfaction (Phil. 3:8)

377 **The Savior's Invitation**

(Mark 10:14)

Command of the Savior

Objectors Silenced by the Word

Many Children have obeyed the Call

Everyone Saved and Happy

378   Threefold Cords

The Way, the Truth, the Life (John 14:6)
Faith, Hope, Love (1 Cor. 13:13)
Grace, Mercy, Peace (2 Tim. 1:2)

379   The Lamb of God

(John 1:29)

Lowly, Loving Savior

Atoning, All-Cleansing Sacrifice

Mighty, Majestic Lord

Beloved, Bountiful Friend

380   Sheep

Straying from God (Isa. 53:6)

Hastening to Death (Ps. 44:11)

Easily Beguiled (Jer. 1:6)

Eagerly Sought (Luke 15:4)

Purchased and Kept (Acts 20:28)

381   The Word

The Incarnate Word (John 1:4)—The Person of Christ
The Quickening Word (John v. 24)—The Word of Christ
The Enlightening Words (Ps. 129:130)—The Holy Scriptures

382   **A Beautiful Text**

(Luke 19:10)

His Name: "The Son of Man
His Mission: is Come to Seek
His Work: and to Save
His Object: that which was Lost"

383   **What Is the Time?**

Time is Short (1 Cor. 7:29)
Time to Awake (Romans 13:12)
Time to seek the Lord (Hos. 10:12)
Time of thy Visitation (Luke 19:44)

384   **The Five Senses**

Smelling a Sweet Savor, God is Satisfied (Eph. 5:2)
Hearing Christ's Words, I get Life (John 5:24)
Seeing Christ's Work, I have Peace (John 20:20)
Tasting that the Lord is Gracious, I am Saved (1 Peter 2:3)
Feeling comes after Faith. I feel because I know (Mark 5:29)

BIBLE CLASS OUTLINES

385   Grace

Sovereign Grace (2 Tim. 1:9)
Saving Grace (Eph. 2:8)
Sustaining Grace (2 Cor. 9:9)
Sufficient Grace (2 Cor. 12:9)

386   More Grace

By Grace, Justified (Rom. 3:24)
In Grace, Standing (Rom. 5:2)
Under Grace, Discipline (Rom. 6:14)
Through Grace, Hoping (2 Thess. 2:11)

387   Peace

Made at Cross (Col. 1:20)
Manifested in Resurrection (Job 20:19, 20)
Mine in Believing (Rom. 5:1)

388   Abundance of Peace

"Perfect Peace," in Trusting God (Isa. 26:3)
"Great Peace," by Loving His Word (Ps. 119:16)
"My Peace," the Gift of Christ (John 14:27)
Peace Always, by all Means (2 Thess. 3:16)

389   Salvation

Salvation Procured by the Death of Christ (1 Cor. 15:2, 3)
Salvation Possessed by Faith in Christ (Acts 16:31)
Salvation Assured by the Life of Christ (Rom. 5:9)
Salvation Perfected at the Return of Christ (Heb. 9:28)

390 Things That Accompany Salvation
(Hebrews 6:9)

Knowledge of Salvation (Luke 1:77)—By the Word
Joy of Salvation (Ps. 51:12)—In the Soul
Strength of Salvation (Isa. 33:6)—By the Spirit
Hope of Salvation (1 Thess. 5:8)—At the Advent

391   Forgiveness

Its Cause—Christ's Death (Eph. 1:7)
Its Blessedness—Expressed in Psalm 22:1
Its Extent—"All Trespasses" (Col. 2:12)
Its Possession—"Hath Forgiven" (Eph. 4:32)
Its Certainty—"Are Forgiven" (1 John 2:12)
Its Effect—Stated in Psalm 130:4

392   Redemption

Accomplished at the Cross—By Blood (1 Peter 1:19)
Experienced at Conversion—By Power (Ps. 104:10)
Expected at the Advent—Of the Body (Eph. 4:30)

393   Eternal Life

A Free Gift from God (Rom. 6:23)
A Present Possession in Christ (John 10:28)
A Glorious Prospect with Christ (Rom. 6:22)

394   The Christian's Standing

Beloved by God, the Father (Rom. 1:7)
Complete in Christ, the Son (Col. 2:10)
Sealed by God, the Spirit (Eph. 1:13)

395   Aspects of Christian Life

Children in God's Family (1 John 3:1)
Servants in Christ's Kingdom (Col. 1:13)
Soldiers in the Battlefield (2 Tim. 2:3)
Strangers in the World (1 Peter 2:11)

396   Our Relations to Christ

United to Christ (Rom. 7:4)—In Life
Abiding in Christ (John 15:3)—In Fruitfulness
Witnessing for Christ (Acts 1:6)—In the World
Glorified with Christ (Rom. 8:17)—In Heaven

397   The Christian's Relation to the World

Chosen out of the World (John 17:6)—by God
Severed from the World (Gal. 1:4)—By the Cross
Sent into the World (John 17:8)—As Witnesses
Shining in the World (Phil. 2:15)—As Lights
Hated by the World (John 17:14)—For Christ

398   Christ for His People

Their Savior to Save (Matt. 1:21)
Their Shepherd to Lead (1 Peter 2:24)
Their High Priest to Succor (Heb. 2:14)
Their Hope to Wait for (1 Tim. 1:1)

399   Christ, Our Keeper

He Keeps His Own (John 17:11)
Keeps them from Stumbling (Jude 24)
Keeps them from Evil (2 Thess. 3:3)

400   Christ, Our Lord

Confessed at Conversion (Rom. 10:9)
Received in Subjection (Col. 2:6)
Obeyed in Life (Col. 3:17)
Acknowledged in Service (Col. 3:24)

401   The Spirit's Work in Believers

Born of the Spirit (John 3:7)—Regeneration
Indwelt by the Spirit (Gal. 4:4)—Sonship
Sealed by the Spirit (Eph. 1:13)—Security
Taught by the Spirit (John 2:24)—Progress

402   Inflow, Upflow, Outflow

The Inflow of the Spirit (1 Cor. 12:13)—Conversion
The Fulness of the Spirit (Acts 7:55)—Communion
The Upflow of the Spirit (John 4:14)—Worship
The Outflow of the Spirit (John 7:38, 39)—Testimony

403   The Coming of Christ

His own Promise (John 14:2, 3)
His Last Word (Rev. 22:20)
The Christian's Hope (1 Tim. 1:1)
The Christian's Attitude (1 Cor. 1:7)

TALKS TO YOUNG CHRISTIANS

404   A Threefold Relationship

Born into the Family of the Father (John 1:12, 13)
Translated into the Kingdom of the Son (Col. 1:13)
Built into the Temple of the Spirit (Eph. 2:22)

405   Christ Is Able

To Save all the Way (Heb. 7:25)
To Deliver from Satan's Power (2 Tim. 4:19)
To Keep till that Day (2 Tim. 1:12)

406   Gospel Blessings

Freely Forgiven (Col. 2:13)
Fully Justified (Acts 13:39)
Finally Glorified (Rom. 8:30)

407   Threefold Security

Safe in Christ's Life (Rom. 5:10)
Kept by God's Power (1 Peter 1:5)
Sealed by the Spirit (Eph. 1:13)

408   What Grace Does

It brings Salvation to the Sinner (Titus 2:11)
It Teaches the Saved (Titus 2:12)
It Strengthens the Servant (2 Tim. 2:1)

409   Three Vital Truths

Chosen by God, the Father (Eph. 1:3)
Redeemed by Christ, the Son (Eph. 1:7)
Indwelt by the Holy Spirit (1 Cor. 6:19)

410   The Christian's Position

Accepted in the Beloved (Eph. 1:6)
Complete in Christ (Col. 2:10)
Joined to the Lord (1 Cor. 6:14)

411   Eternal Life

Life in *Promise* (John 10:10)
Life in *Possession* (John 10:28; 1 John 5:13)
Life in *Prospect* (Titus 1:1; Rom. 6:24)

412   Laws of Spiritual Health

Pure Food (1 Peter 2:2; Jer. 15:16)
Clean Life (Ps. 119:9; Eph. 5:26)
Clear Atmosphere (2 Cor. 6:14-17; 1 John 1:7)
Good Exercise (1 Tim. 4:6; Acts 22:2)

413   Three Relationships

Children in Relationship (1 John 3:1, 2; 1 Peter 1:13)
Saints in Separation (Rom. 1:7; Eph. 5:3)
Servants in Obedience (John 12:24; Col. 3:24)

414   Christ Exalted

As Savior, to Rescue (Acts 5:9; Heb. 7:25)
As Shepherd, to Lead (Heb. 13:20; Ps. 23:1)
As Lord, to Govern (Rom. 10:9; Col. 2:5)

415   The Word of God

As Food to Strengthen (Job 23:12)
As Light to Guide (Ps. 119:103)
As Water to Cleanse (Eph. 5:26)

416   Three Present Blessings

Justified by Faith (Rom. 5:1; Acts 13:39)
Sanctified by Blood (Heb. 10:10; 13:12)
Kept by Power (1 Peter 1:5; John 10:28)

417   The Work of the Spirit

In relation to the Believer

Born of the Spirit of Life (John 3:5; Rom. 8:2)
Indwelt by the Spirit of Sonship (Gal. 4:4; Rom. 8:17)
Strengthened by the Spirit of Power (Eph. 3:16; Phil. 1:10)

418   Without Blemish

Christ, in His Person and Nature (1 Peter 1:19)
Believers, in their Call and Position (Eph. 1:3)
The Church, finally in Glory (Eph. 5:28)

419   Spiritual Life

Imparted at new Birth (1 John 3:1; 5:9)
Developed by Experience (John 6:30; 1 Peter 2:2)
Perfected in Glory (2 Cor. 4)

420   The Christian's Employment

Working in the Vineyard (3 John 4)
Walking in the Truth (Matt. 21:28)
Warring with the Foe (Eph. 6:10-17)

421   Christ for His People

Christ Died for Us (Rom. 5:8)—As Sacrifice
Christ Lives for Us (Heb. 4:13)—As Priest
Christ Comes for Us (John 14:3)—As Hope

422   Three Enemies

The Flesh and its Lusts (1 Peter 2:11)
The World and its Snares (1 John 2:16)
The Devil and his Wiles (Eph. 6:11)

423   A Threefold Cord
(Romans 5:1-2)

Peace through Faith (v. 1)
Standing in Grace (v. 2)
Waiting for Glory (v. 2)

424   Divine Love

The *Father's* Love to His Children (1 John 3:1)
The *Son's* Love to His Church (Eph. 5:25)
The *Spirit's* Love to His Charge (Rom. 15:30)

425   Christ for Me

Christ my Peace (Eph. 2:14)
Christ my Life (Col. 3:4)
Christ my Hope (1 Tim. 1:1)

426   Grace

Saving Grace (Eph. 2:8)—For Sinners
Strengthening Grace (2 Tim. 2:1)—For Servants
Sustaining Grace (2 Cor. 9:8)—For Saints

427   Three Gifts

God's Gift to the World (John 3:16)—His Son
Christ's Gift to His Own (John 17:9)—The Word
The Spirit's Gift to the Servant (Acts 1:7)—Power

428   Looking

Looking *to* Christ (Isa. 45:22)—For Salvation
Looking *on* Christ (John 1:36)—For Example
Looking *for* Christ (Phil. 3:20)—Our Hope

429   Eternal Realities

Eternal Life (1 John 5:13)—In Possession
Eternal Salvation (Heb. 5:9)—In Experience
Eternal Glory (1 Peter 5:10)—In Prospect

430 Keeping Ourselves

In the Love of God (Jude 21)—For Warmth
Unspotted from the World (James 1:27)—For Holiness
From Idols (1 John 5:21)—For Devotion

431 Walk

In Light (1 John 1:7)—Before God
In Love (Eph. 5:2)—With God
In Truth (3 John 7)—After God

432 Spiritual Outfit

Shoes to Walk (Eph. 6:15)
Girdle for Service (Luke 12:35)
Helmet for Warfare (1 Thess. 5:8)

433 Life, Light, and Love

Life Possessed in Christ (1 John 5:11)
Light Received through the Word (Ps. 119:130)
Love Imparted by the Spirit (Rom. 5:5)

434 Practical Christianity

Keep the *Heart* (Prov. 4:23)
Exercise the *Conscience* (Acts 24:16)
Watch the *Tongue* (Ps. 141:3)
Guide the *Feet* (Heb. 12:13)

435 God Well-pleased

In His Beloved Son (Matt. 3:17)
In His Redeemed People (Ps. 149:4)
In their Obedience (Col. 3:20)
With their Sacrifices (Heb. 13:16)

436   The Christian's Hope

An Anchor to Keep (Heb. 6:19)
A Treasure to Love (Col. 1:5)
A Power to Purify (1 John 3:3)

437   The Happy Man

Whose Trust is in the Lord (Jer. 17:7)
Whose Transgression is Forgiven (Ps. 37:1)
Whose Strength the Lord is (Ps. 84:12)

438   The Believer's High Places

Of Security—"In Christ" (Eph. 1:2)
Of Blessing—"With Christ" (Eph. 2:6)
Of Responsibility—"For Christ" (John 13:18)

439   Rewards for Service

Crown of Rejoicing (1 Thess. 2:19, 20)—The Worker's Reward
Crown of Righteousness (2 Tim. 4:6-8)—The Watcher's Crown
Crown of Life (Rev. 2:10)—The Martyr's Crown

440   The Lord's Disciple

The Disciple's Place—The Feet of Jesus (Luke 10:37)
The Disciple's Path—The Example of Jesus (Luke 14:27)
The Disciple's Portion—Rejection with Jesus (John 15:20)

441   The Lord, Thy Keeper

How He keeps His redeemed people

As a *Gardener* his Plants (Isa. 27:3)
As a *Soldier* his Charge (2 Tim. 1:12)
As a *Watchman* his Trust (Ps. 121:4)

THEMES FOR THE ANXIOUS

442 Christ, Our Life

A Truthful Declaration (John 6:53)
A Gracious Invitation (John 7:37)
A Sure Appropriation (1 John 5:12)
A Woeful Lamentation (John 5:40)

443 Christ, Our Peace

He made it at the Cross (Col. 1:20)
He preaches it in the Gospel (Acts 10:36)
He gives it from the Throne (2 Thess. 3:16)
He speaks it to His People (Ps. 85:8)

444 The Love of God

Manifested in the Gift of His Son (1 John 4:9)
Commended in the Death of Christ (Rom. 5:8)
Perceived in the Substitution of Christ (1 John 3:16)
Perfected in Believing on Christ (1 John 4:12)

445 God's Great Salvation

Brought to me in Grace (Titus 2:11)
Received by me in Faith (1 Peter 1:9)
Confessed to others in Testimony (Luke 2:30)

446 God's Earnest Expostulations

God *Commands* all to Repent towards Him (Acts 17:30)
God *Invites,* to Reason with Him (Isa. 1:18)
God *Beseeches,* to be Reconciled to Him (2 Cor. 5:20)

447   Threefold Certainty

Safe, by the finished Work of Christ (John 19:30)
Sure, through the written Word of God (John 1:12)
Sealed, by the Spirit of Promise (Eph. 1:13)

448   The Grace of God

Saves all that Believe (Eph. 2:8)
Justifies all that Trust (Rom. 3:24)
Preserves all who are Saved (1 Cor. 15:10)
Abounds toward all in Need (2 Cor. 9:8)

449   A Great Invitation
(Isaiah 45:22)

A Simple Act—"Look"
A Glorious Person—"Unto Me"
A Great Reality—"And be ye saved"
A Free Invitation—"All the ends of the earth"

450   Cause and Effect

"Not that we loved God, but He loved us" (1 John 4:10)
"Who loved me, and gave Himself for me" (Gal. 2:20)
"We love Him, because He first loved us" (John 4:19)

451   Our Salvation

In Possession, when we Believe (Acts 16:31)
In Progress, as we Continue (Rom. 5:10)
In Prospect, at the Lord's Coming (Rom. 13:11)

452   Our Life

Received at the new Birth (John 20:31)
Assured by the Word of God (1 John 5:13)
Manifested in Daily Walk (2 Cor. 4:11)
Perfected in coming Glory (2 Cor. 5:4)

453   Three Present Blessings
(Colossians 1:12-13)

Deliverance—"Who hath Delivered us"
Translation—"Who hath Translated us"
Meetness—"Who hath made us Meet"

454   Divine Power

Kept by the Power of God (1 Peter 1:5)
Sustained by the Power of Christ (2 Cor. 12:9)
Strengthened by the Power of the Spirit (Eph. 3:17)

455   Eternal Things

A Great Purchase—Eternal Redemption (Heb. 9:12)
A Good Possession—Eternal Life (1 John 5:13)
A Sure Promise—Eternal Glory (1 Peter 5:11)

456   "In Christ Jesus"

Saved in the Living One (Rom. 5:10)
Accepted in the Beloved (Eph. 1:6)
Complete in the Head (Col. 1:10)

457   Our Safeguards

The Peace of God, to Guard (Phil. 4:7)
The Love of God, to Protect (Jude 21)
The Power of God, to Preserve (1 Peter 1:5)

458   A Question and Its Answer

Who can be Saved? (Mark 10:26)
Answer—"Sinners" (1 Tim. 1:15)
        "Any Man" (John 10:9)
        "Thou" (Acts 16:31)

459   Free Forgiveness

For all Men (Acts 13:38)
Of all Nations (Acts 10:43)
Of all Sins (Col. 2:12)

460   Christ Is All

As Savior, He saves from Sin (Matt. 1:21)
As Sanctifier, He sets apart to God (Heb. 2:11)
As Shepherd, He guides the Steps (1 Peter 2:24)

461   Three Positions of the Believer
(Philippians 3)

Found in Christ (v. 9)—His Place
Fellowship with Christ (v. 10)—His Privilege
Fashioned like Christ (v. 21)—His Prospect

462   "No More"

No more Pleasure for Sinners (Job 7:10)
No more Offering for Sin (Heb. 10:18)
No more Remembrance of Sin (Heb. 10:12)

463   Cleansing From Sin

Not by our own Efforts (Jer. 2:22)
Only by Jesus' Blood (1 John 1:7)
Daily by the Word of God (Ps. 119:9)

464   In Christ's Name

Salvation is in His Name (Acts 4:12)
Life through His Name (John 20:31)
Remission in His Name (Luke 24:47)

465   His Own

His Own Self (1 Peter 2:24)—Our Sacrifice
His Own Body (1 Peter 2:24)—Bare our Sins
His Own Blood (Rev. 1:7)—Looses from Sins

466   The Gospel Call

All are Invited (Matt. 11:28)
All things are Ready (Luke 14:17)
All are Welcome (John 6:36)

SUBJECTS
FOR SPECIAL OCCASIONS

THE DEATH OF A CLASSMATE

467   A Folded Lamb

(Isaiah 40:11; Revelation 7:17)

Gathered with the Shepherd's arms—Conversion
Carried in His Bosom—Preservation
Led by the Fountains—Glorification

468   Three Stages of Life's Journey

Redeemed from Evil (Gen. 47:16)—By Blood
Preserved from Evil (Ps. 121:7)—By Power
Taken from Evil (Isa. 57:1)—By Death

469   "With Christ"

Absent from the Body (2 Cor. 5:8)
At Home with the Lord (2 Cor. 5:8)
With Christ, which is far better (Phil. 1:23)

470   Loved Ones Gone Before

They are at Rest (Rev. 14:13)
They are in Paradise (Luke 23:43)
They are with Christ (Phil. 1:23)
They shall rise again (1 Thess. 4:16)

471   Death and Afterward

Death does not end all (Luke 16:19-23)
It is followed by Judgment (Heb. 9:27)
The Resurrection of Judgment (John 5:29)
The Throne of Judgment (Rom. 20:11, 12)

PRIZE DISTRIBUTIONS

472   Great Gifts

God's great Love Gift (John 3:16)—To All
Christ's great Life Gift (1 Tim. 2:6)—For All
The Gift of the Spirit (Acts 10:45)—In all Believers
The Gift of Eternal Glory (John 17:22)—To Saints

473   Gifts and Rewards

The Gift of Grace (Rom. 5:15)—Without Merit
The Gift of Life (Rom. 6:23)—Without Price
The Reward of Iniquity (Acts 1:18)—Wages of Sin
The Reward of Service (Luke 5:35)—For Saints
    The gifts are for sinners, the rewards are for the service of saved ones.

474   Prizes

The Heavenly Prize (Phil. 3:14)—To Press on for
One Receives it (1 Cor. 9:24)—Individual reward
You may lose it (2 John 8)—By unfaithfulness
You may be robbed of it (Col. 2:18)—By Craft

NEW YEAR TREATS AND TEAS

475   Happy Days

The Happy Day of Conversion (Acts 8:39)
Happy Days of Service (1 Kings 10:8)
Happy Days in Obedience (John 13:17)
Happy in the midst of Suffering (1 Peter 4:14)

476   The Heavenly Race and Reward

A Good Start (Acts 9:20)—Clear Conversion
A Clean Stripping (Heb. 12:11)—Of all Weights
A Straight Course (Phil. 3:14)—No Halting
A Good Ending (2 Tim. 4:7, 8)—A Bright Goal

477   Bible Singers

A Solo in the Palace (Ps. 57:7)
A Duet in a Prison (Acts 16:25)
An Orchestra in the Temple (2 Chron. 5:12, 13)
A Chorus in Heaven (Rev. 5:9)

478   Some Scripture Songs

A Song of Redemption (Exod 15:1)
A Song of Deliverance (Ps. 27:7)
A Song of Glory (Rev. 19:5)

479   Shining Lights

As the Sun, Warmly (James 1:11)
As the Star, Brilliantly (Jer. 31:35)
As the Lamp, Humbly (Luke 11:36)
As the Candle, Usefully (Luke 15:8)

TRIPS AND EXCURSIONS

480   The Gospel Railway

Station: The Cross (1 Cor. 1:18)—Where we start
Booking Office: Only One (John 10:9)—All enter
Starting Time: Now (2 Cor. 6:2)—No Alterations
Journey: Comfortable (John 14:15)—Good Conductor
Terminal: Beautiful (Rev. 21:1)—Eternal Glory

481   The Ship of Salvation

Captain: The Lord Jesus (Heb. 2:10)
Crew: Angelic and Human (Heb. 1:14, 6:10)
Passengers: Sinners of all Nations (Acts 15:14)
Accommodation: Large and Healthy (Ps. 31:8)
Port: Eternal Glory (Luke 8:22; 1 Peter 5:10)

FAREWELLS

482   A Parting Promise

(Genesis 28:15)

"Behold, I am with thee" (Matt. 28:20)
"And will keep thee" (Ps. 121:5)
"In all places" (Ps. 139:7-9)
"I will not leave thee" (Heb. 13:5)

483   A Benediction

(Numbers 6:24-26)

"The Lord bless thee and keep thee" (Ps. 29:7)
"The Lord make His face to shine" (Ps. 31:16)
"And be gracious unto thee" (Ps. 30:19)
"The Lord lift up His countenance (Ps. 89:15)
"And give thee peace" (John 14:27)

BIBLE SEARCHING

**For Sunday schoolers, Bible Classes and young folks at home.
An excellent Bible exercise**

484   A Bible Boy to Find

Whose sons obeyed their father's word, and drank on fiery wine?
Whose uncle viewed the promised land and saw its fruitful vine?
Whose house was early turned to God, to serve His people here?
Who followed a rejected King, and sought no land or gear?
Whose Son has told us of the Lord in character as King?
Who walked to Shiloh every year her boy a coat to bring?
  Initals give a Bible Name, who in the days of youth received
  Jehovah's holy Word, and owned it as the Truth.

Answer:—"Josiah" (2 Chronicles 34:2-19).

485   A Royal Searching

Who crowned an orphan, royal queen?
Who took a crown from kingly brow?

What king forsook those who had been
Used to wise monarch's words to bow?

In what fine gold will yet a queen
Be found arrayed in days to come,

When Israel's earthly joys abound,
And under Christ they dwell at home?

Whose king arose from his royal throne,
And clad in sackcloth sat alone?

The capitals when rightly set, produce the honored name of none
Who wore a "golden crown," yet had no kingly reign

Answer:—"Aaron" (Exodus 29:6)

486   A Jumbled Word Searching

The jumbled words, when properly arranged, give the names of Bible
Birds. Fill in chapter and verse where found.

LWOSLWA, Lev. _____   GLEEA, Deut. _____
PAGINWL, Lev._____   SWORPRA, Luke_____
VNEAR, Song of Sol. _____   VOED, Ps. _____

487   A Bible King

Who like a lion seeketh to devour
The sinner saved, in an unguarded hour?

Whose Trade did an apostle daily share,
Content to labor for his daily fare?

What in the Temple was there rent in twain,
To show the way to God is now made plain?
To what great Sin was Israel in the desert prone?
Which robbed the Lord of what was His alone?

Who for his noble faith and fearless stand
Was raised to honor in a heathen land?

Initials name a King; where did he reign?
Who was his friend, in what great battle slain?
Of whom is he a type? Where is it shown
His son will reign upon his father's throne?

Answer-"**David**" (Luke 1: 32).

488   A Bible Town

Where once a baby boy was born.
Where once a widow gathered corn.
Where once a shepherd lad did keep
His father's flock of lambs and sheep.
Give all the places in the word,
Where these events are on record.

Answer-"**Bethehem**" (Matthew 2:1; Ruth 3; 1 Samuel 16)

489   A Bible City

Its first is in Death, but not in Life.
Its second in Warm, but not in Strife.
Its third in Need, but not in Care.
Its whole a place where idols were.

Answer-"**Dan**" (1 Kings 12:29)

490   Bible Towns

Arrange the Jumbled Letters

NAHRMGITMO	ARCNUAPEM	AIHLDEPALGIP
Gathrimmon	Capernaum	Philadelphia

491   A Hidden Text to Find

It is found in the very longest Psalm.

It tells what Luke 15 says I am.

When you learn it, turn to Isaiah 53,

And find what God has done for thee.

Answer—"Lost Sheep" (Psalm 69:176).

492   A Bible Town

It was once a city great and high,
Against which a prophet of God did cry.
Its people on hearing his solenm word,
Repented of sin and turned to the Lord.

Answer—"Nineveh" (Jonah 3:56).

493   A Scripture Town

A much loved Boy of Bible times, and called "a little one."
A lad on whom a "Blessing" came, his father's youngest son.

A Child whose early days were spent in "knowing" God's blest Word,
And who in latter years became a "servant of the Lord."
A Son of God's anointed priest, a "son of Belial," too.

The Eldest Brother of a boy, who once a "champion" slew.
A King whose mother taught him how to plead the needy's cause,
And to avoid the drunkard's cup, and judge by righteous laws.

Initial letters of these words will form a Bible Town,
The place where once a pilgrim came, and weary laid him down
Who dreamed a dream of heavenly bliss while calmly sleeping there
And rose refreshed to know and own Jehovah's tender care.

Answer—"Bethel" (Genesis 28:19).

494   Three Bible Shepherds

Give their names and what each is specially noted for in the Bible.
Their names can be formed from the following letters:
L, D, U, D, E, A, J, A, V, A, I, B, H, D.

Answer—"David" (1 Samuel 16:11); "Abel" (Genesis 4:2);
"Judah" (Genesis 37:12, 26).

495   A Name of God

What man escaped a city's fate,
And once as judge sat in its gate?

Who hid the prophets of the Lord,
And saved them from a woman's sword?

Whose Husband reigned from India's strand
To Ethiopia's barren land?

Whose wife in Shiloh offered prayer,
And also sang God's praised there?

The four initials added, spell a Name of God you know so well

Answer—"**Love**," (1 John 4:8).

496   Bible Acrostic

The Name of Jacob's youngest son? —Gen. 35:18
A Stone that told what God had done? —1 Sam. 7:12
A Saint who showed great unbelief? —John 20:24
One who to God poured out her grief? —1 Sam. 1:20
A Man to save his life who fled? —Gen. 19:17-22
A Queen who filed another's stead? —Esth. 2:7
A King who had God's witness slain? —Matt. 4:1, 10
And One whose prayers stayed the rain? —1 Kings 17:1
Who lived the longest here below? —Gen. 5:27

       Initials give the place you know.

Answer—"**Bethlehem**" (Matthew 2:1).

497   A Man of Prayer

A man of prayer in olden time,
   of honorable name,
Who asked that God might bless and keep
   From every evil claim;
That God would still his coast extend,
   And by His hand himself defend.
Who was the man? Where did he live?
   His history and his service give.

Answer—"**Jabez**" (1 Chronicles 4:10).

498   A Bible Priest to Find

A King by God's true prophet slain?
Who crowned an orphan queen to reign?

Who was great grandma of the King,
Whose psalms and praises still we sing?

Who evil "wrought" before the Lord,
And set at nought His Holy Word?

A King whose pride God did abase,
Who turned to Him and gave Him praise?

Initials form a Bible Name,
A priest of God, of desert fame.

Answer—"Aaron" (Exodus 28:11).

499   A New Testament Word

Where one who served the Church abode,
Who for his pride was smote by God?
Whose words did Absalom disdain?
Who watched her sons in battle slain?
Who mocked his younger brother's claim?
Who from the dead was raised again?
What did King Saul in pieces rend,
And round the coasts of Israel send?

Initial letters all combined produce what suffers and is "kind."

Answer—"Charity" (1 Corinthians 13:4).

500   A Saving Word

A Mount on which a king was slain?

A Bride brought home with camel train?

A Shepherd by his brother slain?

A Brook dried up through want of rain?

A Queen who for her people prayed,

And by her means had judgment stayed?

Initials form a precious word, which those know best who trust the Lord.

Answer—"Grace" (Ephesians 2:8).

INDEX

Other Sermon Outline Titles:

Briggs, S.R. and Elliot, J.H.
600 BIBLE GEMS AND OUTLINES

Jabez Burns Sermon Outline Series
149 SERMON OUTLINES
151 SERMON OUTLINES
199 SERMON OUTLINES
200 SERMON OUTLINES
201 SERMON OUTLINES
91 SERMON OUTLINES ON TYPES AND METAPHORS

Marsh, F.E.
500 BIBLE STUDY OUTLINES
1000 BIBLE STUDY OUTLINES
ILLUSTRATED BIBLE STUDY OUTLINES

John Ritchie Sermon Outline Series
500 SERMON OUTLINES ON BASIC BIBLE TRUTHS
500 CHILDREN'S SERMON OUTLINES
500 EVANGELISTIC SERMON OUTLINES
500 GOSPEL ILLUSTRATIONS
500 GOSPEL SERMON OUTLINES
500 SERMON OUTLINES ON THE CHRISTIAN LIFE

Easy-to-Use Sermon Outline Series
Edited by Charles R. Wood
EVANGELISTIC SERMON OUTLINES
REVIVAL SERMON OUTLINES
SERMON OUTLINES FOR FUNERAL SERVICES
SERMON OUTLINES FOR SPECIAL DAYS AND OCCASIONS
SERMON OUTLINES FOR TEENS
SERMON OUTLINES FROM PROVERBS
SERMON OUTLINES FROM THE SERMON ON THE MOUNT
SERMON OUTLINES ON THE PSALMS